UNIVERSAL ZIONISM

THE MOVEMENT FOR ISRAEL & THE NATIONS

RABBI TULY WEISZ

ISRAƐL365

Universal Zionism

The Movement for Israel & the Nations

By Rabbi Tuly Weisz

Copyright © by Rabbi Tuly Weisz

October 2025

ISBN: 978-1-957109-90-9

Israel365

15 Hamasger Street

Beit Shemesh, Israel

www.Israel365.com

www.Universal-Zionism.com

Dedication

in loving memory of

Peppy and George Weisz ז״ל

Holocaust survivors who emerged from humanity's darkest days carrying unbreakable faith in our brightest possibilities.

Their lives taught that hope is the most defiant and necessary act of courage. They survived and chose to build rather than retreat and to pass on light rather than despair into darkness. Their resilience became our inheritance, and their warm smiles and deep optimism became the guideposts for future generations. This book is written in the spirit they embodied: that the Jewish story, forged in suffering carries within it a universal hope for a better future that we can help create.

May their memory be a blessing.

Am Yisrael Chai

עם ישראל חי

In Memory Of Charlie Kirk

(1993-2025)

*"Love the Lord your God with all your heart
and with all your soul and with all your strength."
(Deuteronomy 6:5)*

*"As for the Nations who attach themselves to the Lord,
To serve Him, and to love the name of the Lord, to be His
attendants,
All who observe the Sabbath and do not desecrate it,
And who hold fast to My covenant,
I will bring them to My sacred mountain
And let them rejoice in My house of prayer.
Their burnt offerings and sacrifices shall be welcome on My altar;
For My House shall be called a house of prayer for all peoples."
(Isaiah 56:6-7)*

Chair of the Religious Zionist Faction

Member of Knesset Ohad Tal

יושב ראש סיעת הציונות הדתית

חבר הכנסת אוהד טל

Dear Rabbi Tuly Weisz,

I would like to offer my congratulations on the release of your new book "Universal Zionism", which profoundly describes the role of the people of Israel as a light unto the nations. As it is written: "I will also make you a light for the nations, that my salvation may reach to the end of the earth" (Isaiah 49:6). Our return to the Land of Israel after two thousand years of exile is not only a national miracle for us, but a mission for all humanity - to be a "kingdom of priests and a holy nation" (Exodus 19:6).

Just as the Kohen (priest) serves the people, so too is Israel called to connect the nations to the Creator. Your book highlights this truth, and strengthens the understanding that Zionism is a global vision. Thanks to people like you, bridges of faith and love are formed between Israel and the nations.

I admire your brave work at Israel365, constantly reminding us of our responsibility to repair the world by connecting humanity to the light of the Torah. May your new book continue to inspire many hearts, and bring blessings to us all.

With great appreciation,

Ohad Tal

Member of Knesset

State of Israel

EAGLES' WINGS

NEW YORK
LOS ANGELES
SÃO PAULO
FRANKFURT
JERUSALEM

Dear Rabbi Weisz,

On behalf of Eagles' Wings, the Israel Christian Nexus, and the millions of Christians worldwide who faithfully support the state of Israel, I want to congratulate you on the important release of your new book "Universal Zionism", a work that is a testament to the vital relationship between Jews and Christians and the urgent importance of an articulate defense of the state of Israel in these challenging times.

The present world we are living in, which has seen an alarming rise of antisemitic incidents and anti-Israel protests at large, is in need more than ever of clear voices who not only stand with Israel but who will also, (despite potential differences in policy or theology), lead the way together in a universal appeal to humanity that confronts the evil of antisemitism at its very core.

The vitality of global Zionism, an integral part of the viability of Israel, constitutes not merely a religious or political issue but an issue upon which rests the future of civilization as we know it. The work of Israel365 is leading the way in uniting people of goodwill around the world in the movement for Israel and the nations, as you have so eloquently illustrated in the publishing of this book.

It is my honor and privilege to stand with you in this holy work on behalf of Israel, so that together we will see the fulfillment of the ancient prophetic scripture which declares, "Come, and let us go up to the mountain of the Lord, to the house of the God of Jacob; He will teach us His ways, and we shall walk in His paths. For out of Zion shall go forth the law, and the word of the Lord from Jerusalem" (Isaiah 2:3).

For Zion's Sake,

Bishop Robert Stearns

DR. ROBERT STEARNS
Executive Director
robertstearns

Eagles Wings • PO Box 450, Clarence, NY 14031 USA
716 759 1058 | office@eagleswings.org
eagleswings.org

CONTENTS

INTRODUCTION

The war that began suddenly on Simchat Torah 2023 ended dramatically on the eve of Simchat Torah 2025. As helicopters carried the last twenty living hostages from two tortured years of captivity in Gaza to hospitals in Israel, President Donald Trump arrived in Jerusalem to deliver a victory speech to a packed Knesset.

The peace president opened his historic remarks in the most appropriate of ways:

> "Mr. Prime Minister, Mr. Speaker, esteemed members of the Knesset and cherished citizens of Israel, we gather on a day of profound joy, of soaring hope, of renewed faith, and above all, a day to give our deepest thanks to the Almighty God of Abraham, Isaac, and Jacob...

> Generations from now, this will be remembered as the moment that everything began to change, and change very much for the better. Like the USA right now, it will be the golden age of Israel, and the golden age of the Middle East."

This book will attempt to describe the spiritual-political path to achieving that golden age, the very path set out by the Almighty God of Abraham, Isaac and Jacob.

President Trump was in the Middle East for less than 24 hours before racing halfway across the world back to Washington to deliver his nation's highest honor, the Presidential Medal of Freedom, to Charlie Kirk on what would have been his 32nd birthday.

Just four weeks earlier, as students returned to campus for the fall 2025 semester, Charlie Kirk prepared for another college tour. The media star loved meeting students, sharing his faith, and talking about America's role in preserving western civilization. In the years since founding Turning Point USA, Charlie had become a fixture on college campuses throughout America, debating students with his friendly invitation to "Prove Me Wrong."

On Tuesday, September 9th, the day before embarking on his "America's Comeback Tour," Charlie invited a few friends and advisors to sharpen his arguments on what had become, to his chagrin, an increasingly contentious topic: Israel. He wanted to know the facts and the best ways to debunk the fake news and lies spreading fast across social media, so he organized a Zoom call to review common questions one last time before boarding his flight to Utah the next morning.

Since the outbreak of the Israel-Hamas war on October 7th, 2023, students had grown increasingly vocal in their opposition to the Jewish State, and this pained Charlie deeply. He had spent years articulating a vision for the world based on conservative values, and Charlie saw America's support for Israel as a critical ingredient in the glue holding American morality together. After all, Israel - the nation-state of the Jewish people - represented the "Judeo" part of the Judeo-Christian values that Charlie cared so deeply about. To Charlie, Israel couldn't simply be removed from the system without the rest unravelling.

Alarmed by the corrosive impact of social media manipulation on young American students, in May 2025, Charlie sat down and wrote a detailed letter to Israel's Prime Minister.

> "One of my greatest joys as a Christian is advocating for Israel and forming alliances with Jews in the fight to protect Judeo-Christian civilization. Most recently, I am proud to have taken over Ambassador Huckabee's show on TBN where we continually support Israel and the Jewish people. As Muhammadism spreads into Western societies, it's critical that Jews and Christians stay united in the effort to contain and roll back radical Islam and Sharia law. I regret to report that anti-Israel and anti-Semitic trends are at record levels on social media. These negative sentiments then flow downstream into college campuses and even seep into the conservative MAGA community.

> My team and I have spent months analyzing these trends and debating ideas that could help you and your country pushback against these disturbing developments. Anti-Israel sentiment can undermine American support for Israel. The purpose of this letter is to lay out our concerns and outline potential remedies. Everything written here is from a place of deep love for Israel and the Jewish people..."

The Zoom call wrapped up after about an hour, and Charlie shared a thought with the small group of Christians and Jews, Americans and Israelis he had gathered. "You know, it feels like we have this tent with four pillars holding everything up: America and Israel, Jews and Christians. If one of those pillars comes down, so will all of western civilization."

On Wednesday, September 10th, Charlie boarded a flight from Arizona to Utah Valley University. It would be his last. He was shot by an assassin while doing what he loved most, engaging students with a smile on his face, under a tent that read "Prove Me Wrong."

This book is dedicated to Charlie Kirk, whose death a month before his 32nd birthday proved that it isn't about how many years you live, but how you live those years. It is not meant to claim his legacy as primarily that of a Zionist, although he certainly was one. Rather, it stands as a token of appreciation for his being the best example of this book's central topic: Universal Zionism.

Universal Zionism describes the golden age of Israel and the world, the next stage of the Zionist movement - one that is outward-facing and meant as much for non-Jews as for Jews. Universal Zionism calls for Jews to build meaningful relationships with Christians, grounding those relationships in shared biblical values rooted in the Torah, and celebrating shared institutions such as the Sabbath.

As a teenager, Charlie recognized that America was heading in the wrong direction and, despite his youth and inexperience, dedicated himself to reversing that course. With an abundance of kindness and charisma, he organized America's largest grassroots movement of young people committed to faith, family, and freedom. Charlie's Christianity gave him a spiritual-political perspective that enabled him to see clearly the dangers facing western civilization, particularly the Red-Green alliance of Marxists and Islamists.

Self-taught and brilliant, Charlie learned from everyone around him, but was especially close with an older mentor and the two formed a world changing relationship. Charlie met Dennis Prager when he was a teen, and became Prager's number one fan. The love was mutual and Dennis, a committed Jew, generously gave of his professional wisdom and media platform while also sharing his personal love for the Torah and Jewish practices, including the beauty of Shabbat. Just before he was killed, Charlie had just finished writing a book that he dedicated to Dennis Prager called "Stop in the Name of God: Why Honoring the Sabbath will Transform Your Life." The book, posthumously, became a bestseller and has ignited unprecedented non-Jewish interest in the Jewish Sabbath.

The special relationship between Charlie and Dennis demonstrates the vital importance of building meaningful relationships between Christians and Jews. This book will argue that Jewish-Christian reconciliation is the most vital alliance of our generation - one that will lead to the restoration of Israel, America, and the world.

Charlie cared deeply about Israel and was proud to be one of the Jewish State's most vocal advocates. In his letter to Prime Minister Netanyahu, Charlie urged the government to launch an "Israel Truth Network" to fight the lies and misinformation while articulating Israel's narrative more effectively. I am proud that Israel365 was selected to develop and launch the Israel Truth Network in memory of Charlie, following in his footsteps by defending truth and fighting for the survival of western civilization.

Charlie's assassination was both a violent assault on our values and a psychological attack in the clash of civilizations he constantly warned about. Within hours of his shocking murder, social media exploded with horrific accusations blaming Israel and the Jews - the very people who loved Charlie most - while Israel's enemies shamelessly celebrated. This blood libel represents exactly the kind of propaganda warfare Charlie fought against throughout his life.

Yet Charlie's vile murderer will not succeed in silencing his voice. As this book will demonstrate, God uses devastating tragedies and major setbacks as launching points for great revolutions. The Jewish people suffered their worst catastrophe during the

Holocaust, yet three years later, with the establishment of the State of Israel in 1948, they launched a period of growth, creativity, and development unseen since biblical times.

Theodor Herzl, another legend whose writings are still studied long after his own untimely death at the age of 44, once observed, "The idea is for the community what bread and water are for the individual." This book develops the idea that our generation hungers and thirsts for. Universal Zionism represents the culmination of a story that has been unfolding for millennia, written in the pages of history and foretold in the world's most influential book, the Bible.

Two years of unprecedented military and propaganda warfare have brought clarity to this moment in history. The October 7th attacks and the global response that followed have done more than test Israel's military capabilities - they have revealed the strength of the Jewish State's alliances. At the same time, the war has exposed the fault lines that divide civilization from barbarism and unmasked all those who stand in the way of peace and prosperity. What is emerging from this crucible is a crystallization of political and spiritual partnerships that will define the next era of human history.

Thanks to its deep foundations, the strength of the US-Israel relationship, while being tested under the most extreme conditions, has held up. Beyond the close military and intelligence cooperation, however, we witnessed something deeper: the recognition that Israel and America, Jews and Christians - the bearers of Charlie's four civilizational tent poles - share strategic interests and a common destiny rooted in the same cherished values and principles.

Simultaneously, those who celebrated terrorism, who chanted for Israel's destruction in the streets of London, Paris, and Melbourne, and who turned university campuses into platforms for hatred, exposed themselves with sickening clarity. They have removed their masks, and the world can now see which side stands for life and which side celebrates death, which ideologies build and which seek only to destroy.

Progressing to the next stage of history will require more than military victory or diplomatic success. It will require a big idea powerful enough to inspire people across nations, faiths, and cultures. That elusive idea is hidden in plain sight, waiting to be rediscovered through a simple, honest reading of the Bible.

The Bible undoubtedly has earned its status as the most influential book in human history. More copies have been printed, more languages have carried its words, more art has been inspired by its stories, and more lives have been transformed by its message than any other text. People across every continent know its stories and have looked to it for guidance throughout the centuries. Yet when it comes to understanding Israel, nearly everyone still has it wrong.

Universal Zionism is the expression of ancient Biblical ideals made relevant for our contemporary world. It represents both a political movement and a religious revival - an invitation to discover how Israel's story holds the key to solving humanity's deepest challenges. It offers a path to make the greatest impact in the lives of Jews and non-Jews but by aligning with God's will and the arc of history itself.

The Bible tells mankind's story through three central elements: the God of Israel, the Land of Israel, and the People of Israel. Genesis opens universally - the creation of the world and humanity's experience in Eden establishes that all people share a common origin and purpose. Then it narrows its focus to follow one specific family, using their particular story to illuminate universal truths.

British Chief Rabbi Jonathan Sacks explained this pattern:

> "God is universal, religions are particular. Religion is the translation of God into a particular language and thus into the life of a group, a nation, a community of faith. In the course of history, God has spoken to mankind in many languages: through Judaism to Jews, Christianity to Christians, Islam to Muslims. Only such a God is truly transcendental - greater not only than the natural universe but also than the spiritual universe articulated in any single faith, any specific language of human sensibility."

After establishing Himself as Creator, God makes specific promises to one family. He tells Abraham: "All the land that you see, to you will I give it, and to your seed forever." He repeats this promise to Isaac and then to Jacob, binding this family eternally to a specific piece of land. The family becomes a tribe, and the tribe becomes a nation. They endure slavery in Egypt, experience divine revelation at Mount Sinai, and eventually enter their promised land where they establish the Kingdom of Israel under kings Saul, David, and Solomon.

This kingdom becomes the focal point through which humanity's destiny unfolds - through the messianic promise of a son born to the House of David who will transform the entire world.

While the Bible chronicles the story of the Jewish people in rich detail, it was never intended to be only for Jews. What makes the Bible so eternal is its way of using particular stories to teach universal truths. Paradoxically, the best way to speak to all of humanity is through the experience of one people.

THE BIBLE'S GOLDEN AGE

The Torah describes a golden age. Surprisingly, it's not the generation of the Garden of Eden, despite its perfect harmony between God, mankind, and nature. Instead, the Torah points to an even greater era - the reign of King Solomon.

Scripture speaks of this golden age when everyone was "dwelling securely, every man under his vine and under his fig tree" (1 Kings 4:25). This was not merely an era of material prosperity, but a moment when the knowledge of God spread outwards, when nations streamed to Jerusalem seeking wisdom, and when the Temple Solomon built became a "house of prayer for all Nations" (Isaiah 56:7).

Kings came from distant lands to hear Solomon's wisdom. Trade routes connected Israel to civilizations across three continents. Peace reigned not through conquest but through the mesmerizing might of righteousness and wisdom. For a brief, shining moment in history, the world glimpsed what human civilization could become when aligned with God's purpose.

Yet Solomon's golden age didn't last.

The wise king made critical mistakes. He accommodated foreign gods to please his many wives, imposed heavy taxes that burdened his people, and allowed the spiritual foundation built by his father David to erode beneath the weight of material success. The kingdom divided, the Temple was eventually destroyed, and the people were scattered to the four corners of the earth.

But the prophets saw further. Isaiah, Micah, Amos, and others described a future era that would surpass even Solomon's own times. The children of those sent into exile would return from the ends of the earth, they would turn the barren wasteland into lush fields and vineyards, Jerusalem would be reestablished as the moral capital, nation would not lift sword against nation, and the earth would be full of the knowledge of the Lord as waters cover the sea (Isaiah 2:2-4, 11:9).

Central to this prophetic vision was Israel's destined role as "a light unto the nations," as Isaiah (42:6) writes, "I the Lord have called thee in righteousness, and have taken hold of your hand, and kept you, and set you for a covenant of the people, as a light unto the nations." The restoration of the Jewish people to their land was never meant to benefit Jews alone - it was to illuminate a path for all humanity. The prophet envisioned a time when Israel's return would demonstrate God's faithfulness to all peoples, inspiring the nations to seek the wisdom and justice that flow from Jerusalem. This universal mission, embedded in the prophetic texts for millennia, awaits final fulfillment in our generation.

After October 7th, we are now positioned at the threshold of an era even greater than the golden age of Solomon. We have the historical perspective that the wise king lacked, the technological capabilities his era couldn't imagine, and the ability to learn from his errors. The modern State of Israel, emerging against impossible odds and thriving despite constant violent opposition, provides the foundation for the conclusion of history's greatest story.

Universal Zionism tells the story of Israel's exciting progression, a trajectory based on the biblical kings of Israel and elevated by the heroes of modern Jewish history. However, this is not a book about the past.

The structure of this book follows the rise, achievements, and limitations of Israel's three most famous kings: Saul, David, and Solomon. By understanding what made each king unique and learning from their lives, we can avoid repeating key mistakes while building upon their successes. Each monarch corresponds to a specific phase of modern Israeli history and Zionism, the movement for Jewish national restoration.

We will see how Political Zionism led to Religious Zionism, and how we are currently moving towards Universal Zionism.

We will trace the incredible development of Political Zionism through leaders who achieved what was considered impossible: the return of the Jewish people to their ancestral homeland after two millennia of exile.

We will explore the inspirational teachings of Religious Zionism, which recognized that political independence without spiritual renewal would be as incomplete as a body without a soul.

Finally, we will explain why the third stage - Universal Zionism - requires the active collective effort of Jews and gentiles to seize the moment to achieve what history has been building toward for thousands of years.

Each king had a unique historical mission that parallels the challenges facing contemporary Israel:

King Saul sought the security and normalization of his people, responding to the Israelites' explicit demand, "That we may be like all the other nations, let our king rule over us and go out at our head and fight our battles" (1 Samuel 8:20). Political Zionism pursued identical goals: the normalization of the Jewish people among the nations and the security that comes from having a homeland to defend. We will see how political Zionist legends like Theodor Herzl, David Ben-Gurion, and Benjamin Netanyahu each contributed essential elements to this foundation.

King David prioritized the Jewish people's spiritual foundation, leading a national religious revival that culminated in bringing the Ark of the Covenant back to Jerusalem. When "David danced before the Lord with all his might" (2 Samuel 6:14), he demonstrated that true strength comes not from military power alone but from spiritual vitality. We will discuss the pioneers of Religious Zionism, whose courage in challenging long-held assumptions energized the Zionist movement with spiritual passion. We will also examine their ideological opponents and explore where Religious Zionism has lost momentum.

King Solomon's mission was to spread the notion of the One God to all mankind, culminating in the construction of the Temple, a "house of prayer for all Nations" that drew worshippers from across the known world. However, Solomon could reach such heights only because he stood on the shoulders of David's spiritual renaissance, which itself rested on the political and military stability that Saul had established.

Each stage builds upon the foundation established in the preceding one. King David could ignite a spiritual renaissance in the nation only because King Saul had created the stable political and military framework that made internal growth possible. King Solomon could fulfill his universal mission only by leveraging the spiritual depth and internal strength that David had fostered throughout his reign.

The progression from one phase to the next required profound shifts in the kingdom's priorities and policies: from securing national survival, to cultivating spiritual vitality, to embracing a universal mission. Such sweeping transitions inevitably created tensions between outgoing and incoming leaders. Each king experienced strained relationships with his successor, often showing reluctance to acknowledge or empower the next phase, and sometimes even acting with outright hostility.

King Saul, for instance, repeatedly attempted to kill David, recognizing intuitively that David's spiritual approach would supersede his purely political methods. King David delayed naming Solomon as his heir until a power struggle with his son Adonijah forced his hand, requiring urgent intervention from Bathsheba and the prophet Nathan to secure the succession.

These historical patterns repeat in our modern era with remarkable precision. The pioneers of Political Zionism achieved unprecedented success: they brought Jews back from the four corners of the earth, drained malaria-infested swamps and made deserts bloom, created a world-class innovative hub, and built one of the world's most capable armies.

The leaders of Religious Zionism, despite facing great opposition, identified ideals that captured the imaginations of both Jews and Christians, inspiring both faiths to rethink basic and long-held assumptions about their relationship to each other and to the Land of Israel. These two great faiths are now closer than at any point since the first century, recognizing their shared stake in Israel's success and their common opposition to forces that seek to destroy them both.

The reconciliation between Jews and Christians represents the crucial first step, but it is not where Universal Zionism will end. The reason this book focuses on the relationship between Jews and Christians specifically is because these two faith traditions share a uniquely strong foundation for unity, which will inevitably spread outward to all of humanity.

Yet, for the moment, vicious opponents of Israel are an increasing threat to the world. The dangers they pose are growing and spreading faster than ever, amplified by technology, social media, and artificial intelligence that can spread disinformation at unprecedented scale and speed. The battle for hearts and minds has moved to digital battlefields, where truth and falsehood compete in real-time for global influence. Sadly, as Winston Churchill observed, "A lie gets halfway around the world before the truth has a chance to put its pants on."

But this crisis also presents an unprecedented opportunity. If we can learn from ancient kings and modern prime ministers, from courageous religious leaders who are willing to rethink and revise long-held beliefs, then we can achieve the original covenant and promise made to humanity through Abraham: "In you all the families of the earth shall be blessed" (Genesis 12:3).

The choice before us is stark and the window of opportunity may not be open for long. We can seize this moment to fulfill history's greatest promise, or we can allow fear, division, and shortsightedness to squander the chance to achieve what previous generations could only have dreamed about.

MY PERSONAL JOURNEY

This book is not a personal memoir, yet I will draw upon my life experiences to illustrate my own progression from Political to Religious to Universal Zionism.

I grew up in an Orthodox family in Columbus, Ohio, attending Jewish day schools and Zionist summer camps throughout my childhood. My paternal grandparents were Holocaust survivors, a reality that shaped my upbringing and worldview in ways that have similarly deeply affected many third-generation descendants. Ever since I was a kid, I heard stories from my grandparents about Auschwitz, resilience, faith in God and commitment to Judaism. The shadow of the Shoah was never far from our dinner table conversations, and helped shape my understanding of what it meant to be Jewish in the modern world.

My maternal grandparents, Ruth and Rabbi David Stavsky were pillars of the Jewish community in Central Ohio, leaders who built institutions and bridges that would serve generations. The small but vibrant Jewish community of Columbus provided a complete ecosystem. We had our own schools, our own grocery stores, our own social circles, our own world. As a child in the 1980s, I was fascinated by Israel and devoured every book on its history that I could find in the public library or second-hand bookstores.

I was particularly mesmerized by Theodor Herzl, the founder of Political Zionism, who almost single-handedly birthed the audacious idea of a Jewish State. Here was a man who looked at two thousand years of exile and persecution and declared, "If you will it, it is no dream."

I read about the remarkable feats of Israel's prime ministers: Ben-Gurion's bold declaration of independence despite overwhelming odds, Golda Meir's steely determination during the Yom Kippur War and Menachem Begin's journey from underground fighter to Nobel Peace Prize winner. I was inspired by Israel's scrappiness and success - the way a tiny nation surrounded by enemies had not only survived but flourished, and even as a youngster took personal pride in the Jewish State's achievements.

My wonderful parents encouraged my passion for Israel and passed down their own deep connections to the country. My mother was given by her parents an exotic sounding Israeli name, Chanita. She had spent a year studying in Jerusalem when she was a teenager and, as a young mom, was a beloved teacher in Hebrew School at one of the local synagogues.

My father Michael was named after both of his grandfathers who were killed in the Holocaust. As the only son, when his parents asked how he would like to celebrate his Bar Mitzvah, he answered with an audacious request: a trip to Israel. My grandparents, Peppy and George Weisz, could hardly afford it, but for them, my father was their pride and joy, so they agreed. When they arrived at the Western Wall, my grandmother broke down crying, remembering how her own mother in Europe would pray for the restoration of Israel. She could never have imagined her descendants celebrating in Jerusalem.

When I turned thirteen, my parents took me and my three younger sisters on our first family trip to Israel, to commemorate my own Bar Mitzvah. I remember getting called to the Torah, standing in front of the Western Wall and feeling the weight of history in those ancient stones. The connection was immediate and powerful. Israel was *Home*, even though I had never been there before.

After high school, I spent a transformative year studying Torah in a yeshiva (seminary in Hebrew) just outside of Jerusalem. There's an ancient rabbinic saying that "the air of the Land of Israel makes one wise" and I fell in love with studying the "Torah of Eretz Yisrael" - the unique style of Jewish learning that could only fully flourish in the land where it all took place. Concepts that had seemed abstract in America came to life in vivid color when studied in Israel. Studying the prophets wasn't boring when you could walk through the City of David, or visit any of the same places that others could only read about.

I decided to spend a second year of study in yeshiva, where along with dozens of other young men from the States, I studied Torah from early morning until late at night with few distractions. I was discovering a worldview that saw every current event, every historical development, every personal decision as part of a grand divine narrative leading toward spiritual redemption. If while growing up in America, I absorbed the lessons of Political Zionism, having tasted Israel, I was beginning to sense that there was more out there and starting my journey into Religious Zionism.

After completing my intensive Israeli yeshiva experience, I continued my Judaic and university education in New York, earning both a law degree and rabbinical ordination from Yeshiva University (YU). The synthesis of secular and sacred learning was meant to uniquely instill a proud Jewish identity combined with full engagement in the modern world, and I tried to embrace it all.

During the Second Intifada in 2003, Yeshiva University organized a solidarity trip to Israel for their students. On that powerful experience, 100 young men and 100 young women visited terror victims recovering in hospitals and volunteered in Israeli schools. Ordinarily, YU has separate campuses for men and women, and so I must admit that we also enjoyed the mixed buses, which is where

I met my future wife, Abby. Abby raised up the energy level of the whole trip, and with her contagious smile and magnetic personality brought great cheer to those whose spirits we had come to uplift. It wasn't for another year, but on the following winter break, we both found ourselves again in Israel. We had our first date in Jerusalem where we both immediately knew that we were soulmates.

Once Abby had finished two masters degrees, in social work and Jewish education, we spent a year in Jerusalem where I completed my rabbinic ordination. It was a joy to be studying Torah again in Israel, and a magical way to begin our marriage. During that period, I received the invitation of a lifetime. I was called by my home community to become the rabbi of the same synagogue where my grandfather had served for close to fifty years.

My grandfather, Rabbi David Stavsky, was a legend. Born in the Lower East Side of New York City, he too went to Yeshiva University. It was in the years following the Holocaust and America found itself at war again. Instinctively, he immediately left his studies to enlist in the US army during the Korean War. My grandfather was inspired to follow in the footsteps of his older brother who served in World War II. Once the war finished, Chaplain Stavsky was recruited to the Beth Jacob Congregation in Columbus. He arrived in 1956 along with my grandmother Ruth, and dedicated all of his tremendous skills to the Jewish community there. Over the many years, Rabbi Stavsky not only served his congregation, he built a Jewish day school and many other essential institutions. I felt incredibly fortunate stepping into his role as the young rabbi of the congregation where I had grown up.

Though my work as rabbi of a large synagogue with hundreds of families was demanding, I found time to serve on the boards of different local community organizations. Ironically, it was through my activities on behalf of the Jewish community that I came to know Christians for the first time in my life.

Growing up in our Jewish bubble, my interactions with faithful Christians had been virtually nonexistent. The two faith communities lived parallel lives in the same city, but in complete silos with minimal meaningful contact.

At one meeting at the Columbus Jewish Federation in 2008, we heard a presentation from a Christian Zionist - which at the time I thought was a complete oxymoron. The pastor wearing jeans and a cowboy hat piqued my interest, and we ended up speaking in the parking lot for hours after his talk. He opened up a whole new world for me.

Columbus had ten synagogues, and having lived there my whole life, I pretty much knew everyone in the Jewish community. I learned that there were over one thousand churches in Columbus and thousands of local Christians who loved Israel as much as we did, and I didn't know any one of them!

At first I was skeptical, but that led to curiosity and I quickly met some of the local clergy and began speaking to Christian groups about Judaism and Israel. What I found was simply astonishing. Over and over again, I met Christians from my own hometown who prayed for the peace of Jerusalem each day. I could not believe how many Evangelicals knew their bible and supported Israel with a passion exceeding that of many Jews!

Christian Zionism existed throughout the United States. I just had never heard of it, and neither had practically any of my rabbi friends. When I started looking into this phenomenon, many of my colleagues in the Jewish community expressed skepticism and dismissed my curiosity as naive. "Don't you know," they warned me patronizingly, "all Christians just want to kill us or convert us." Their reaction was understandable given Jewish history, but it wasn't consistent with the actual people I had been getting to know. Clearly something fundamentally different was happening right in front of our eyes, but the Jewish community wasn't paying attention.

LIVING THE DREAM

As our family grew, Abby and I felt that Israel was calling to us, quietly at first, then more insistently. We loved America and were building a wonderful life in Columbus, but began fantasizing about raising our own children in the land of our forefathers. In 2011, we finally made Aliyah. Moving across the world and away from extended family is always a dramatic change, and giving up the wonderful life of pulpit leadership took considerable adjustment. What I didn't anticipate was how intensely my worldview would change during our first years in Israel.

Breathing the air of Jerusalem, drinking water that flowed through biblical valleys, and experiencing daily life with Jews from dozens of countries contributed to an overwhelming sense of spiritual rebirth. Abby and I and our three young kids took it all in with a glorious sense of wonder. We prayed at the Western Wall, celebrated the festivals where our ancestors worshiped, planted trees where our people had worked the land, participated in funerals for soldiers who paid the ultimate sacrifice, and marveled at how quickly our children were absorbing Hebrew - much faster than their parents!

The most festive confirmation of our decision to make Aliyah came when two of my three sisters moved to Israel with their own families. More than half of our family was suddenly living in Israel as ancient prophecies about the ingathering of the exiles weren't abstract concepts any longer, but our lived reality. We were active participants in the rebirth of the Jewish people in our ancestral homeland. We were living the dream and loving every minute of it.

Abby and I both felt that the spirit of Israel was entering our physical bodies, filling empty spaces we hadn't even realized existed. In America, my head had understood the importance of having a Jewish State; in Israel, my heart experienced what it meant to be organically attached to our homeland. Although I didn't use the terminology at the time, I was transitioning from a Political Zionist to a Religious Zionist, and the transformation was both gradual and sudden, like watching the sun rise over the horizon.

One of my most treasured memories from our first years in Israel captures the nature of the process we are experiencing. My two oldest daughters wanted to experience sunrise over the Sea of Galilee, that ancient body of water where so much history had unfolded. And so, one spring morning during Passover, we set out in the pre-dawn darkness to hike up Mount Arbel, the towering cliff that overlooks the entire Galilee basin.

The climb was steep and challenging in the darkness. But then, slowly, the first rays of light began to appear over the eastern horizon. The mountains of Jordan, ancient Moab and Ammon, began to emerge as silhouettes to the east and the mountains of the Golan Heights took shape to the north. As the sun crept higher, its rays sparkled across the waters of the Sea of Galilee, transforming the entire landscape into brilliant clarity.

Standing there with my daughters, I was reminded of a Talmudic teaching that occurred at that very spot. Two great sages of the first century, Rabbi Yehoshua and Rabbi Eliezer, were debating the nature of Israel's ultimate redemption. Would it come suddenly, like a lightning bolt splitting the sky, or would it unfold gradually, like the dawn? Rabbi Yehoshua remarked, "Just as the light of dawn appears over the valley of Arbel slowly, slowly (*"kimah kimah"* in Hebrew), so too will the redemption of Israel unfold slowly, slowly."

As we stood on Mount Arbel watching this ancient metaphor come to life before our eyes, it finally hit me. The return of the Jewish people to our land, the rebuilding of our homeland, the ingathering of the exiles from the four corners of the earth, all of this has been unfolding *kimah kimah*, slowly, slowly, just as Rabbi Yehoshua had prophesied. Standing there with my girls, I realized that just like our history, our future would unfold the same way. More and more people around the world would begin to open their eyes to what we could already see from that mountaintop - that Israel's light is meant to illuminate not just the Jewish people, but all of humanity.

FROM THE BEGINNING TO THE END OF THE YEAR

One practice that pushed us toward Israel was my daily Bible reading, a good habit I picked up during my years of study in yeshiva. When I finally read through the entire book, I was struck by how much the Torah is actually about the land of Israel - more than anything else.

There were so many beautiful passages about Israel that I began typing up my favorite ones in a spreadsheet. One verse in particular touched my heart: "The land you are going to is not like Egypt...it is a land the eyes of your Lord are upon from the beginning of the year till the end of the year" (Deuteronomy 11:12).

For some reason, I couldn't stop thinking about God focusing on Israel every day. That verse became the foundational scripture for Israel365, the organization I founded to focus our eyes and hearts on Israel each day of the year. After a few months of settling in and completing Ulpan (a Hebrew language immersion course), I sent the first Israel365 email newsletter on January 1, 2012 - "from the beginning of the year" - and we have grown every day since then.

Though I didn't yet fully understand what I was starting, we had 10,000 email subscribers join in our first month and 100,000 subscribers by the end of our first year. I was thrilled that Israel365 had quickly become one of the primary ways that Jewish and Christian Zionists engaged each day with the land and people of Israel. By contributing to charitable and humanitarian projects and staying educated through *The Israel Bible* website and *Israel365 News*, hundreds of thousands of people worldwide were connecting daily with news and inspiration from Israel.

Having traded a congregation of Orthodox Jews for an online community of mainly Evangelical Christians, I started thinking more deeply about Jewish-Christian relations. The history was messy from the start. Jesus and the apostles were Jewish, but Christianity developed a framework that saw itself as having replaced Judaism in God's plan. This "Replacement Theology" led to a tragic history: Crusades, Inquisitions, pogroms, and ultimately the Holocaust.

But something unprecedented was happening in our time. While there had always been exceptional gentiles who refused to follow the crowd, never before had masses of Christians looked positively toward Jews. Many in the Jewish community questioned why a nice Jewish boy would dedicate his life to working with Christians. But I was convinced we were experiencing something new and profound. It felt like God was bringing His fractured family back together after centuries of separation.

THE NIGHTMARE OF OCTOBER 7TH

My extended family was celebrating the joyous Simchat Torah holiday in 2023 at my sister's house when at 6:29 AM, a strange siren pierced the quiet holiday morning air. At synagogue a few hours later, we immediately recognized that something was catastrophically wrong when, all at once, the young men who were dancing with the Torah scrolls began racing to their cars while still wearing their prayer shawls. Orthodox Jews don't drive on Shabbat or holidays and the sanctity of the day was shattered by the dawning recognition that our lives might be in immediate, mortal danger.

Only after Simchat Torah concluded did we begin to comprehend the magnitude of the tragedy that was unfolding. Initially, we heard reports of fifty people kidnapped from the communities near Gaza. That number soon jumped to one hundred, then two hundred, finally the news announced that two hundred and fifty two people were kidnapped. Another twelve hundred Jews were murdered in the most brutal fashion imaginable. It was a nightmare unfolding before our very eyes, the largest massacre of Jews since the Holocaust and the greatest devastation for the Jewish people since the establishment of the State of Israel.

What proved even more shocking than the October 7th attacks was the global response that began on October 8th. We had always known that Hamas wanted to instigate another genocidal Intifada and annihilate Israel; it was explicitly stated in their founding documents and charter. What was more shocking, however, was how quickly and enthusiastically much of the world rallied to their cause.

In cities with the largest Jewish populations - New York, London, Paris, Sydney - mobs of local activists were suddenly donning keffiyehs, waving Palestinian flags, and screaming "Globalize the Intifada!" If this wasn't terrifying enough, rather than expressing outrage at this sudden explosion of Jew hatred, much of the mainstream media provided admiring coverage of the protests and the campus encampments. Momentum only continued to build as organized mobs all over the world began to attack Jews in the street, vandalize synagogues and cemeteries in ways that were horrifyingly reminiscent of 1930s Europe.

Then the situation deteriorated even further. While Israelis united as never before under the existential threat of a seven-front war, and began to grasp the threat that Palestinian nationalism posed to Israel's very legitimacy, the international movement supporting Hamas only gained strength.

Countries that had decades of diplomatic ties and close coordination with Israel began turning on the Jewish State in the worst way possible - by calling for a Palestinian State. Already in November 2023, US Secretary of State Antony Blinken started calling for a Palestinian State in speech after speech as the official Biden administration policy, leading European countries to follow suit. Before Israel had even fully mobilized its military response, an organized movement to reward Palestinian terror had emerged.

As Israelis struggled to come to grips with the terrible consequences of ceding Gaza to the Palestinian Authority, the international elites began to lecture Israel. According to their perverse logic, October 7th had proven that the only way to end the war was to resurrect the failed Two State Solution, a plan that would create a terror state in Israel's biblical heartland of Judea and Samaria.

The anti-Israel cancer metastasized with frightening speed. Attacks weren't coming only from the usual suspects of left-wing progressives and liberal supporters of the Palestinian cause. Prominent voices on the political right, including many who had long claimed to be stalwart supporters of Israel, were suddenly joining the haters or falling conspicuously silent.

As the war dragged on, political support for Israel, which had been growing steadily for decades, began to reverse. Pastors who had always proclaimed themselves pro-Israel simply stopped talking about the Gaza War, fearful of alienating their younger parishioners and reluctant to appear out of touch or irrelevant.

The golden era of Jewish-Christian relations that I'd spent over a decade working towards seemed to be crumbling before my eyes.

Leaders we'd counted on disappeared when we needed them most. Replacement Theology was making a comeback. I began questioning everything I'd worked for. Maybe my critics were right - maybe Jews really couldn't count on Christians after all?

I wrestled with these doubts while trying to calm our children during daily sprints to our bomb shelter, now stocked with food and provisions. But somewhere in those dark moments, I realized the answer was precisely the opposite: non-Jews were no longer the problem, they were an essential part of the solution.

I started to understand that unlike before, Jewish Zionism and Christian Zionism could no longer exist in separate silos. They had to be brought together, and the alliance between Jews and Christians needed to be dramatically accelerated.

While doing everything we could at Israel365 to provide for the humanitarian needs of war widows and orphans and to support the brave IDF soldiers, we also shifted our organizational focus from Bible education to Israel advocacy. Israel is famous for its military prowess and notoriously infamous when it comes to telling its story through public diplomacy. We felt we had to step in and help fix this critical gap.

Our incredibly dedicated staff threw themselves into advocacy efforts to help Israel communicate its narrative more effectively. We organized hundreds of leading pastors and rabbis into a group called "Keep God's Land" advocating for Judea & Samaria. The fight for sovereignty had become the core issue defining Israel's legitimacy over the entire land. After all, if Israel couldn't defend its connection to Hebron or Bethlehem, key cities in the Biblical tradition, then we have even less of a claim to the modern cities of Herziliya or Tel Aviv.

Additionally, we formed a party called Israel365 Action within the World Zionist Organization, the institution established by Herzl in 1897. Israel365 Action was set up to advocate for Judea and Samaria along with strengthening relations with Christian allies within the official Zionist movement. The bureaucratic work was tedious and the election campaign extremely competitive, but we felt that the symbolism was powerful: we were using Herzl's own institutional framework to advance the next stage of the Zionist movement.

Alongside our advocacy efforts, I began immersing myself deeper than ever in Torah study and the ideological evolution of the Zionist movement. The intensity of our national crisis demanded more than the same, reactive responses. It required a fundamental understanding of the forces at work in history and our moment in the grand narrative.

Having carefully studied the Tanakh (Hebrew Bible) to prepare *The Israel Bible*, which Israel365 published in 2018, I reread it with special focus on the passages describing warfare and the settlement of the land. Ancient texts that hadn't always seemed very important suddenly pulsed with contemporary relevance.

Who is Amalek in our generation? The Torah commands us to "remember what Amalek did to you" and to "blot out the remembrance of Amalek from under heaven" (Deuteronomy 25:17-19). Was this merely ancient history, or was Amalek a recurring enemy that manifests in each generation through those who seek to destroy the Jewish people precisely when we are closest to fulfilling our destiny?

Were the prophecies of Zechariah meant to guide our contemporary decision-making? The prophet's words seemed to describe our current battles with uncanny precision: nations gathering against Jerusalem, Israel standing alone, divine intervention at the moment of greatest peril. "I will gather all the nations against Jerusalem to fight against it... Then the Lord will go forth and fight against those nations" (Zechariah 14:3). These words, written over two millennia ago, read like today's headlines.

What could we learn from our biblical warrior kings that would guide us through contemporary challenges? King Saul's battles with the Philistines, David's urge to unite the Nation and build a home for God, and Solomon's wisdom and expansion of the kingdom were inseparable dimensions of the same cosmic struggles we were experiencing today.

I studied Herzl's writings exhaustively, not just his famous manifesto *The Jewish State*, but his diaries, his correspondence, his novels, and the transcripts of the early Zionist Congresses. I read what his contemporary critics had said about him, both Jewish and non-Jewish voices that dismissed his vision as impossible fantasy or dangerous delusion. The parallels to our current moment were striking: then, as now, the majority of both Jews and gentiles couldn't perceive the historical forces that were already in motion.

I reviewed Rav Kook's revolutionary texts with fresh eyes, studying not only his mystical insights about the spiritual significance of the return to the land, but also what his opponents had argued. Many Orthodox leaders of his era had denounced him as a heretic for suggesting that secular Zionists could be unwitting agents of divine redemption. Other Jews had dismissed him as a relic of medieval thinking who didn't understand modern nationalism. Both sides had missed the profound synthesis Rav Kook was proposing.

Through this intensive research, my understanding of Zionism began shifting once again. I began to perceive patterns that were remarkably clear once I knew how to look for them, like discovering the hidden image in an optical illusion that suddenly becomes impossible to unsee.

Everything we were experiencing had been spelled out in the Torah and was recurring in historical cycles that followed predictable rhythms. The growing onslaught against Israel and the Jewish people weren't random aberrations or temporary setbacks. As painful as they are, attacks on God's chosen people and promised land are a necessary part of the redemptive story, meant to motivate us in ways that peacetime never could. Opposition wasn't evidence that we were off course; it was confirmation that we were approaching our destination.

Antisemitism, I realized, was not the problem but rather a symptom of a deeper dynamic at work. Jew-hatred throughout history has been God's method of preventing the Jewish people from losing our way and forgetting our unique purpose and destiny. It is also the most reliable indicator of a morally sick civilization approaching its own demise.

A cursory review of Jewish history reveals that wherever Christian societies embrace Replacement Theology and turn against the Jews, their own downfall follows with remarkable speed. The Roman Empire began its terminal decline shortly after making Christianity the state religion and implementing anti-Jewish legislation. Medieval kingdoms that expelled their Jewish populations soon found themselves economically and intellectually impoverished. Modern European nations that enthusiastically participated in the Holocaust were themselves destroyed, their cities reduced to rubble, their nations ruined, their populations decimated.

The explosion of antisemitism and support for Hamas unleashed on October 8th might indeed lead to increased persecution of Jews in the short term. But God has made an eternal promise never to abandon Israel: "For the Lord will not forsake His people for his great name's sake" (1 Samuel 12:22). Those countries that allow antisemitism to metastasize, however, have no such guarantee. Their societies will ultimately collapse under the weight of their own moral blindness, just as every antisemitic civilization throughout history has collapsed before them. The correlation is not coincidental. It is structural, spiritual, and inevitable.

GOD'S MOST REPEATED PROMISE

Universal Zionism emerges from the recognition that the Jewish return to Israel is not merely intended to provide a shelter from persecution, or even a spiritual home for Jews to thrive unperturbed by outside forces. Israel's return is the ultimate fulfillment of God's most repeated promise as revealed in the Bible, designed to unleash His greatest blessings upon the entire world. When that plan is blocked, His blessings stop. But when this process advances, those nations and individuals who have supported Israel will be blessed abundantly, and humanity will finally emerge into its greatest era.

The promise made to Abraham, that "I will bless those who bless you, and whoever curses you I will curse; and all peoples on earth will be blessed through you" (Genesis 12:3) was never meant only for Abraham's immediate descendants. The election of Israel represents the divine blueprint for how God's blessing and curse would operate throughout history. Cities, countries and civilizations that align themselves with the Jewish people receive divine favor that manifests in moral clarity which leads to cultural vitality, innovation and prosperity. Those who embrace world views that oppose the Jewish mission in the world will ultimately find themselves fighting against the current of history itself, and will inevitably be swept away. "The Lord will cause your enemies who rise against you to be defeated before you" (Deuteronomy 28:7).

Rather than interfering with God's plan, when Jews and non-Jews align with the mission to restore the people of Israel to their land, we become active spiritual partners with each other and with God. The epic conflict between Jew and gentile that has characterized most of history begins to dissolve. Although it is a process, Christians are realizing that Jewish restoration in Israel actually enables the nations to fulfill their own mission in the world.

This is why Universal Zionism matters as much to a Christian in Kentucky as to a Jew in Jerusalem - maybe more. The Israeli Jew already lives with the blessing that comes with returning to his land. But Christians worldwide can also tap into that same blessing without leaving home. They don't need to move to Israel to play a role in history's greatest story. They simply need to align with the forces working for civilization's advancement rather than its destruction.

Jews are meant to be in Israel in order to follow the Torah, for only in the land can they serve God completely.

> "For you are to cross over the Jordan to go in to take possession of the land that the Lord your God is giving you. And when you possess it and live in it, you shall be careful to perform all the statutes and the rules that I am giving you today." (Deuteronomy 11:31–32)

Although Judaism is viewed as a religion, it is more precisely a nation. The "statutes and the rules" given by Moses are designed not only to meet the needs of a religious community, but of a nation in the process of ordering its governing institutions. Only in Israel can the Jewish people reconstitute themselves as a nation to develop the full force of their creativity and accomplish their historical mission of bringing all the other nations closer to the One God.

Since biblical times, when the Jewish people stray from their mission, Divine Providence allows their enemies to remind them to return - both literally to their land and figuratively to their calling. This cycle appears as the central theme throughout the Book of Judges: Israel prospers, becomes comfortable, begins assimilating with surrounding nations, forgets its distinct mission, falls under foreign oppression, cries out to God, experiences divine rescue through a judge or prophet, returns to its purpose, and the cycle begins again.

The modern period has seen the miracle of Israel's rebirth combined with Jewish communities around the world reaching levels of influence, creativity, and prosperity that would have been unimaginable to previous generations. The current awakening, triggered by October 7th and the global response of October 8th, has the capacity to bring more Jews back to Israel and to bring all of humanity into proper relationship with the divine plan that has been unfolding since the beginning of history.

Rather than responding to all the accusations leveled against us or focusing obsessively on the antisemitic symptoms manifesting all around, Jews must stay focused. We must remember why we are back in Israel in the first place, where we are headed as a nation, and what role we must play in the unfolding of history and human destiny. The major opposition we face from our enemies is not evidence of failure, it is proof that we are approaching success on a scale so magnificent that the forces of evil are marshaling everything they have for one final attempt to prevent it.

Universal Zionism, therefore, represents more than just the next stage of Jewish national development. It provides the ideological framework for humanity's transition into the golden age that has been promised since the beginning of time.

This is the progression I have lived through personally. From Political Zionism (the recognition of the necessity of Jewish statehood) to Religious Zionism (understanding the spiritual significance of the return to the Land) to Universal Zionism (embracing Israel's mission to bring divine light to all nations). My individual journey from America to Israel, from working with a Jewish congregation to building bridges with Christians, from witnessing October 7th to studying and now explaining Universal Zionist ideology, mirrors the collective journey of the Jewish people from exile to return, from isolation to partnership, from being history's victims to becoming the protagonists in the final act of the redemption.

After two years of unprecedented military and propaganda warfare between the forces of light and darkness, we stand at an unprecedented crossroads. The choice before us will determine not only Israel's future, but the future of human civilization itself. Will humanity recognize the divine pattern that has been unfolding for millennia and align with it, ushering in an age of unprecedented blessing and prosperity? Or will we continue to fight against the current of history, experiencing the chaos and destruction that always result from opposing divine will?

The events since October 7th have forced this choice into stark clarity. There are no neutral positions remaining. Every nation, every institution, every individual must choose. Our choices will determine whether our children inherit a world of unprecedented peace and prosperity, or whether they face the collapse of everything previous generations built. The choice could not be clearer, the stakes could not be higher, and the time for decision could not be shorter.

Universal Zionism is not just an idea, it is an invitation and an opportunity to participate in the unfolding of biblical prophecies in the most important story ever told. We have the privilege to be part of the solution to humanity's deepest problems, and to help usher in the golden age that has been promised since the beginning of time.

WHAT UNIVERSAL ZIONISM IS NOT

Before I explain what Universal Zionism represents, it's crucial to clarify, what it is not.

Unlike virtually every other country where Jews lived throughout the diaspora, the United States - founded on biblical principles by deeply religious Christians - has provided Jews with unprecedented freedom, prosperity, and security. Christianity remains the strongest moral force upholding traditional values in

America today. Christians believe in God, study the Bible, and educate their children in its values, building their communities accordingly. Churches are the main force pushing back against the anti-God and anti-biblical ideologies that threaten the foundations of western civilization.

The Jewish flourishing in Christian America stands as powerful testimony to what becomes possible when a nation's dominant faith honors rather than persecutes the Jewish people. This reality must inform how we approach the next stage of Zionism - not with suspicion toward Christianity, but with gratitude and a commitment to strengthen the alliance that has already blessed both our peoples.

Universal Zionism is based on a Jewish appreciation of Christianity, but it is not universalism in the traditional sense. Secular universalism claims that we are all fundamentally the same, that no people should be more entitled to a nation or land than any other, that all distinctions are artificial constructs that should be eliminated. Secular universalism is the empty promise that John Lennon sang about, "Imagine there's no countries, nothing to kill or die for, and no religion too."

The vision of a world without distinct nations, borders or religious differences may sound blissful, but it is the exact opposite of Universal Zionism. God created different peoples with different missions, different lands with different purposes, and different faiths with different roles to play in the ultimate redemption. The goal of Universal Zionism is not to eliminate these distinctions but to harmonize them in service of God's higher purpose.

Although it advocates for a Jewish-Christian alliance, Universal Zionism does not argue in favor of any merger of Judaism and Christianity. While we can and must learn from each other, each side of the Judeo-Christian relationship brings distinct and unique strengths to the partnership, which are essential to preserve. History warns us against eliminating boundaries between our two faiths.

Theodor Herzl himself, despite his genius in envisioning the Jewish State, fell into this trap. Growing up as an assimilated Jew without proper religious guardrails, Herzl had suggested at one point that Jews should convert en masse to Christianity to solve the age-old "Jewish problem." His theological confusion had implications within his own family - his son Hans later converted to Christianity. As a tragic result, the great Zionist leader has no Jewish descendants alive today.

As we begin to cooperate more deeply, we must insist that Jews should remain committed Jews and Christians should remain committed Christians. Through my work at Israel365, and to the dismay of some of my Christian friends, I have worked hard to prevent Christian proselytizing of Jews. Thankfully, I have achieved important results in this regard, which I am very proud of, because maintaining Jewish distinctiveness is essential to God's plan. We can work together, not by weakening our own identity but by strengthening it while building relationships upon mutual respect and shared purpose. Each faith will come to better understand its own role while recognizing how both serve the same ultimate divine plan for humanity's redemption.

Universal Zionism draws inspiration from a revolutionary shift that transformed Judaism in the 20th century. Rabbi Menachem Mendel Schneerson (1902-1994), known as the Lubavitcher Rebbe, or the "Rebbe," repositioned Judaism during the second half of the 20th century from an inward-facing to an outward-facing movement. In the process, he launched a renaissance of Jewish life around the world that continues to this day.

For centuries, Judaism had been primarily concerned with preserving itself, maintaining its traditions, and surviving in hostile environments. The Rebbe taught that the time had come for Judaism to turn outward and share its light with the world.

Chabad Houses were founded in cities across the world, reaching out to unaffiliated Jews while simultaneously engaging with non-Jewish communities in ways that elevated everyone involved.

Universal Zionism applies this same principle to the Zionist movement. Instead of focusing exclusively on Jewish needs, Jewish security, and Jewish prosperity, we must recognize that Israel's flourishing is meant to bless all nations. To be sure, there are already many incredible examples of Israeli outreach to assist impoverished countries and noteworthy emergency response, but Universal Zionism calls for a major reframing of global outreach unlike anything we've seen before.

Universal Zionism does not argue that Herzl's Political Zionism is dead or that Rav Kook's era of Religious Zionism has passed. Redemption is not something new that replaces what came before - it builds methodically on everything that preceded it. This is a movement of construction, not destruction, representing the culmination of all previous stages, not their negation.

Theodor Herzl during the Fifth Zionist Congress in 1901 in Basel (Ephraim Moses Lillien)

In fact, the vision of Universal Zionism was implicit in Zionism from its very inception. Theodor Herzl, focused as he was on the first stage and the urgent task of building Political Zionism, nevertheless understood that the ultimate goal was outwardly focused and for the benefit of the whole world.

In his introduction to *The Jewish State*, Herzl wrote:

"The Jews who wish for a State will have it. We shall live at last as free men on our own soil, and die peacefully in our own homes. The world will be freed by our liberty, enriched by our wealth, magnified by our greatness. And whatever we attempt there for our own benefit will redound mightily and beneficially to the good of all mankind."

In his novel *Altneuland*, Herzl made this universal vision even more explicit: "I am not ashamed to say, though I may expose myself to ridicule in saying so, that once I have witnessed the redemption of the Jews, my people, I wish also to assist in the redemption of the Africans."

Rav Kook and Ben-Gurion, each in their own way, grasped the same truth that Jewish sovereignty was never meant to be an end in itself, but rather the essential foundation for fulfilling Israel's ancient mission to become a blessing to all the families of the earth. What we call Universal Zionism is simply the fulfillment of what these visionaries understood all along - that the three stages of Zionism form one continuous arc toward humanity's ultimate redemption, the restoration of Israel and the world.

Our generation is extraordinarily fortunate to stand on the shoulders of giants, those towering figures who came before us, from Kings Saul, David, and Solomon in ancient times, to Theodor Herzl, Rav Kook, the Rebbe and countless other visionaries who prepared the way for this moment. Universal Zionism honors their legacy by completing what they began, fulfilling the vision they glimpsed but could not yet fully realize. Each previous generation laid essential foundations that make our current moment possible. Now it is our responsibility to build the final story on those foundations, by bringing it to its intended completion.

History reveals a sobering pattern about the rise and fall of great powers. Economic and political superpowers, seemingly invincible in their time, have remarkably short lifespans when measured against the sweep of human history. Venice dominated global commerce in the sixteenth century, the Netherlands ruled the seas in the seventeenth, France shaped European politics in the eighteenth, and Britain commanded a global empire in the nineteenth.

Each of these powers appeared unshakeable at their height. Their currencies were the gold standard of international trade, their militaries were feared across continents, their cultures were emulated by aspiring nations, and their political systems were studied as models of success. Yet each eventually declined, their influence waned, their empires dissolved, and their moment of dominance passed into the history books. Economic superpowers last perhaps two to three centuries at most and political superpowers rarely survive more than four or five centuries. Even the greatest military empires eventually crumble under the costs of maintaining their dominance, and the inevitable rise of new challengers.

Israel is poised to emerge as a great power not only for spiritual reasons, but for historical ones. The Jews lived under nearly every civilization in history, and learned the strengths that each had to offer and the weaknesses that have led to their downfall. Having seen the rise and fall of the Egyptian, Assyrian, Babylonian, Persian, Hellenistic, Roman Empire, Russian, Ottoman, and British Empires, we have seen first hand the drivers that have led to the success of the empires which we will want to incorporate in the next great phase for Israel and the world.

Judaism has survived for 4,000 years precisely because it contains eternal truths that transcend the temporary advantages of economics and politics. Its survival through millennia of persecution, exile, and attempted destruction demonstrates that there are forces in history more powerful than armies and more enduring than wealth. The Jewish people have been strengthened in spite of adversity, unified rather than scattered by diversity, and refined rather than corrupted by the pressures that have destroyed countless other civilizations.

This remarkable endurance stems from Judaism's foundation on Divine truth rather than human ambition, on moral law rather than political expediency, and on spiritual purpose rather than material accumulation. These eternal principles provide stability and resilience that no purely human institution can match and are ready to be unleashed on the world.

A NEW KIND OF SUPERPOWER

The propaganda war against Israel is evidence that nefarious forces are exploiting antisemitism in order to foment division in the West. Yet, these manipulations are being exposed and will have the opposite effect. When the dust settles, many will recognize that Israel has been at the forefront in the epic battle of good over evil and hostility towards Israel will turn into admiration. "In place of your being forsaken and hated, I will make you an everlasting pride, the joy of every generation" (Isaiah 60:15). Part of the post war plan must include major efforts to solidify the Judeo-Christian alliance through education and relationship building.

By highlighting its destined true role in the world, Israel can emerge from the Gaza war not merely as another regional military power or economic success story, but as something unprecedented in world history. Israel can become the world's first moral superpower that combines material strength with spiritual authority, political influence with ethical leadership, and regional dominance with global inspiration.

This will be a paradigm shift from previous Middle Eastern power structures, which have been based either on tribal dominance, religious coercion, or the artificial boundaries imposed by colonial powers. Instead, Israel can establish a new framework based on principled strength and power exercised but in service of higher moral purposes. This means using our military capabilities to protect innocent civilians, leveraging our economic success to lift up our impoverished neighbors, and employing our technological innovations to solve global problems.

Such a transformation will usher in the era of Universal Zionism as a period when Israel's approach to governance, innovation, ethics, and international relations becomes the standard that other nations aspire to emulate. Just as we speak of Greek civilization's contributions to philosophy, Roman civilization's impact on law, and western civilization's influence on democracy, the era of Universal Zionism can be civilization's decisive breakthrough into an era of unprecedented peace and prosperity.

We possess both the power and the ethical authority to fundamentally reshape our region. The IDF has proven its qualitative superiority against multiple adversaries simultaneously. The Israeli economy has demonstrated resilience and innovation that other Middle Eastern nations can only envy. Our democratic institutions have maintained stability and legitimacy while neighboring countries have experienced revolution and chaos.

But most importantly, we have the moral credibility that comes from being the region's only democratic society that truly protects religious minorities, guarantees individual rights, and operates under the rule of law. This gives us something no previous Middle Eastern power has possessed: the ability to lead through attraction rather than coercion and through inspiration rather than intimidation.

Following the war's conclusion, Israel will face a crucial strategic choice that will determine not only the Jewish State's future but the future of the region and world. We must resist the natural temptation to retreat inward, to focus exclusively on our own recovery and reconstruction, to build higher walls and stronger defenses while ignoring the larger possibilities that our victory will have created.

Instead, we must seize this unprecedented opportunity to forge a new identity based on spiritual leadership and global inspiration. This means taking active responsibility for shaping the Middle East's future rather than simply reacting to threats as they emerge. It means using our moment of maximum strength and credibility to establish frameworks that will prevent future conflicts rather than merely preparing to fight another day.

If we choose the path of Universal Zionism - using our success to bless others while maintaining our own strength and identity - we can create a regional transformation that will be studied and emulated around the world. If we choose isolation and self-focus, we will waste an opportunity that may not come again for generations. The question is whether we have the vision and courage to fulfill our potential as the world's first spiritual superpower.

We live in an era when neutrality is impossible and silence is complicity. The forces of chaos and destruction have declared war on everything decent and sacred. They have shown their hand through the barbarism of October 7th and the global celebration of evil that followed on October 8th. The battle lines are drawn, and there is no middle ground.

This book is written for those who refuse to be spectators in history's greatest drama. It is call to action for Jews who understand that their destiny is inextricably linked to Israel's success and for Christians who recognize that their faith's future depends on aligning themselves with the Jewish state. It is for all people of conscience who grasp that Israel's victory will determine whether civilization advances to unprecedented heights or collapses into darkness. We stand at a crossroads where every day of delay and every moment of hesitation moves us further from the golden age that is within our grasp. This is not a time for academic debate or theoretical discussions. This is a time for urgent, decisive, transformative action.

The window of opportunity is closing because the enemies of civilization are mobilizing and the red-green alliance is gaining strength. But so are the forces of light, if we have the courage to act upon the truths revealed in these pages. Universal Zionism calls each of us to join the movement powering the Jewish-Chrstian alliance that will determine whether our children inherit a world of unprecedented peace and blessing, or the collapse of everything previous generations built.

This book provides bold steps to launch the movement for Israel and the nations, but before we determine where we are going, we need to understand where we are now and how we got here. How is it that Zionism, which commanded such widespread respect and admiration at the dawn of the 20th century, now faces such relentless opposition in the 21st? How did the word "Zionist," once embraced with pride by Christians and Jews alike, suddenly become a derogatory term in so many circles on the left and on the right?

The answers to these questions lie not in recent headlines or contemporary politics, but in understanding the remarkable journey that brought us here. We must trace the evolution of an idea that began as a desperate response to persecution and has developed into humanity's greatest hope for redemption.

POLITICAL ZIONISM

2

POLITICAL ZIONISM

After being elected Prime Minister for his sixth term in 2022, Benjamin Netanyahu sat down with Bari Weiss of *The Free Press* for a revealing rapid-fire interview.

> BW: Bibi Netanyahu, a quick lightning round. Who's your political hero?
>
> BN: Theodor Herzl.
>
> BW: Who's your biblical hero?
>
> BN: King Saul. He was tragic.
>
> BW: What's your favorite novel?
>
> BN: My favorite novel? I don't read novels. I read history.
>
> BW: What's your favorite history book?
>
> BN: The Bible.

In those four brief answers, Netanyahu revealed the essential elements for understanding Universal Zionism: Theodor Herzl, King Saul, history, and the Bible. These represent the foundational pillars upon which the Zionist movement was built and the framework through which we can understand where it must go next.

While Netanyahu's identification with Herzl makes sense, his choice of King Saul is baffling. Here stands a man who has led Israel longer than any prime minister, who has steered the nation through multiple wars and diplomatic crises, who has transformed Israel into a regional powerhouse - yet he identifies not with the triumphant King David or the wise King Solomon, but with King Saul, whose reign ended in failure and madness.

This choice may reflect more than political philosophy; it suggests a deeper spiritual lineage. Theodor Herzl's Hebrew name was Binyamin, linking the founder of modern Zionism to the tribe of Benjamin - the same tribe that produced Israel's first king. King Saul was Benjamin's most famous descendant, and like his ancient namesake, Benjamin Netanyahu seems to perceive a thread connecting three Benjamins across time: the biblical king, the Zionist visionary, and himself. It is a lineage marked not by unbroken success, but by the burden of being first - of bearing responsibility in the face of impossible odds, of courageously making decisions that could be judged harshly by history, and of leading a people who remain perpetually divided over their leader's legitimacy.

Like Saul, Netanyahu understands that his primary mission is not the religious elevation of David or the universal outreach, but the fundamental task of ensuring Jewish survival. Like Saul, he faces enemies on all sides who seek the annihilation of his people. And like Saul, Netanyahu recognizes that his own role, however crucial, is ultimately transitional, preparing the ground for something greater that must come after him.

THE BIBLICAL VIEW OF HISTORY

Before we can properly understand King Saul's significance for modern Israel, we must first grasp how the Bible itself views history - a perspective fundamentally different from both ancient and contemporary worldviews.

Although the Torah is not a history book, it instructs us to contemplate historical events. When Moses commanded the Israelites to "Remember the days of old, understand the years of each generation" (Deuteronomy 32:7), he wasn't simply asking them to memorize dates and events. He was teaching a revolutionary way of seeing human history - not as random chaos or endless cycles, but as a purposeful journey with divine direction. Moses continues, "Ask your father, and he will tell you; your elders, and they will instruct you."

The biblical approach to history stands in stark contrast to secular perspectives. In early cultures, history was typically viewed as an endless repetition of recurring patterns without ultimate purpose, like the weather that moved predictably from winter to spring to summer to fall, only to begin the cycle anew. Kings rose and fell, empires expanded and contracted, civilizations flourished and declined, but nothing fundamentally changed or progressed toward any ultimate goal.

In modern secular thought, history is often seen as either the random result of accidents, coincidences, and unforeseeable events, or determined by impersonal forces like economics, technology, or politics. Marxists view history as driven by class struggle, capitalists by market forces, and social scientists by demographic trends. From a secular perspective, human agency and divine purpose are either minimized or eliminated entirely.

The Jewish view offers something radically different. History is the unfolding of a divine-human partnership, a spiritual journey with a clear beginning, purposeful middle, and predestined ending. This belief has profoundly shaped western civilization through the Jewish and Christian traditions, giving meaning to suffering, purpose to struggle, and hope for ultimate resolution.

In this framework, wars, migrations, rises and falls of empires, and even individual decisions by leaders are part of a larger pattern that becomes visible only when viewed from a spiritual-political perspective. The destruction of the First Temple led to the Babylonian exile, which produced the Talmud and preserved Judaism for the future. The Roman destruction of the Second Temple led to the diaspora, which spread Jewish ideas throughout the world. The Spanish expulsion of 1492 scattered Jews to new lands where they would eventually contribute to the Renaissance and Enlightenment. Even the Holocaust, incomprehensible in its evil, led to the rebirth of Israel and the ingathering of the exiles.

Understanding history through this lens is essential for appreciating both the threats and opportunities facing the modern Jewish state. Israel has no greater enemy than forgetfulness, which is why Jewish tradition places such overwhelming emphasis on historical memory. *Zakhor*, remember that God created the world, and that He rescued us from Egypt. Do not forget what the evil Amalek did to you in the wilderness. Remember Jerusalem.

This biblical framework for understanding the past provides the lens through which we can recognize the parallels between our ancient challenges and contemporary struggles. To understand the war thrust upon Netanyahu's Israel on October 7th, we must turn to the origins of the first Jewish government, established three thousand years ago by King Saul, whose reign marked a revolutionary turning point in Israel's history.

LONG LIVE KING SAUL!

During King Saul's reign, the Jewish people transitioned from a loose confederation of twelve tribes governed by judges to a centralized monarchy. The specific circumstances that brought Saul to power bear striking similarities to those that would eventually produce modern Political Zionism.

Following their entry into the Land of Israel by Joshua in around 1400 BCE, the Israelite tribes faced an overwhelming enemy. The Philistines, represented everything that opposed the Jewish mission in the world. Long before the modern-day Palestinian Arabs rejected and provoked Israel, the Philistines posed a constant, persistent, terrifying threat to the Israelites for centuries. The Bible describes them as a tool that God used to test Israel when the people turned away from Him. "And the children of Israel again did that which was evil in the sight of the Lord; and the Lord delivered them into the hand of the Philistines for forty years" (Judges 13:1).

While predominantly controlling the coastal areas of Gaza, Ashkelon and Ashdod, the seafaring Philistine armies made inland inroads as well. They controlled the strategic Jordan Valley in the center of the country and established strongholds in the Judean hills. Most devastatingly, in the 11th century BCE, they captured the Ark of the Covenant from the Israelites. Built by Moses during the wilderness wanderings and housed in Shiloh for centuries, the Ark was Israel's most sacred object - the physical manifestation of God's presence among His people.

The Philistine advance threatened the entire Israelite confederation. Faced with this existential crisis, the tribal chiefs convened under Samuel, the last and greatest of the judges. What decades of civil wars and internal conflicts had failed to accomplish, the Philistine threat achieved almost overnight: unity among the twelve tribes.

This pattern would repeat itself throughout Jewish history. An external enemy forces internal unity. Persecution creates clarity about Jewish identity and purpose. Our enemies inadvertently strengthen the very people they seek to destroy. The Philistine threat forced the Israelites to transcend their tribal divisions and think for the first time as a single united nation.

The task of uniting and defending this emerging nation fell to an unlikely candidate: Saul, son of Kish, a shepherd from the tribe of Benjamin. The choice was remarkable for several reasons. Benjamin, descended from the youngest son of Jacob, was not a large or leading tribe. "Am I not a Benjaminite, from the smallest of the tribes of Israel?" an incredulous Saul asks Samuel (1 Samuel 9:21). Not only that, but the small tribe had been almost wiped out just two generations earlier in a disastrous civil war with the other tribes (Judges 19-21). Yet this history of near-destruction and remarkable resilience may have been precisely what qualified Benjamin to produce Israel's first king.

The prophet Samuel, guided by divine instruction, saw in Saul's background a symbol of hope for tribal unity. If the smallest and most vulnerable tribe could produce a leader capable of defending all of Israel, then perhaps the long festering divisions and jealousies that had weakened the confederation could finally be overcome.

NORMALIZATION AND SECURITY

When the people of Israel approached the prophet Samuel requesting a king, their priorities were clear. They wanted two things above all: normalization and security. "That we may be like all the other nations," they declared, "let our king rule over us and go out at our head and fight our battles" (1 Samuel 8:20).

This demand reflected a deep psychological need that would resurface within the Jewish people throughout history, into the modern era. After generations of feeling different, isolated, and vulnerable, the Israelites yearned to be "like all the other nations," to have the same political structures, military capabilities and national normalcy that their Philistine, Amalekite and Moabite neighbors took for granted. They were tired of being exceptional and relying solely on divine intervention for their defense. They were exhausted of the anxiety-provoking uncertainty that came with their hallowed status as God's chosen people.

The desire for a king represented not only political reorganization, it was a cry for dignity, respect, and the ability to defend themselves like all others in their region. The Israelites wanted to stand as equals among the nations, to be taken seriously as a political entity, to have the power to protect their families without constantly depending on individual judges or miraculous interventions. Eventually, God and Samuel agree to their request and following the special anointing ceremony, "all the people shouted and said, 'Long live the king!'" (1 Samuel 10:25)

King Saul was a reluctant leader thrust into power - who literally stood "head and shoulders taller than all the people" (1 Samuel 10:23). Throughout his reign, he remained a populist focused relentlessly on the practical necessities of statecraft: building institutions, organizing armies, defending borders, and establishing Israel's credibility as a regional power. Saul demonstrated for all time that Jewish survival required Jewish power, and Jewish power required Jewish statehood.

King Saul organized Israel's first standing army, moving beyond the ad hoc militias that had served under the judges. He achieved significant military victories against multiple enemies, fighting successful campaigns against the Philistines, Moabites, Edomites, and Amalekites, securing Israel's borders. He won crucial battles that broke his enemies' momentum and restored Israelite morale. His military campaigns provided Israel with breathing room from the constant foreign oppression that had characterized the period of the judges. By rallying the Israelite tribes to fight as one nation rather than as separate entities, Saul fostered a stronger sense of national unity and shared destiny.

"Saul consolidated the kingdom over Israel" (1 Samuel 14:47) and achieved remarkable success in his mandate. His anointment by Samuel gave divine legitimacy to this new institution of kingship, creating a precedent that would endure for centuries. Saul began the process of creating a royal court and governmental bureaucracy, including officials, military commanders, and scribes. He centralized religious and political authority, laying essential groundwork for the more sophisticated administrative systems that David and Solomon would later develop.

At the same time, Saul's reign revealed the inherent limitations of a Jewish king focusing exclusively on political and military objectives. Spiritual pursuits were simply not his priority, and when religious obligations conflicted with political necessities, he consistently chose the latter- which ultimately led to his tragic demise.

His first mistake occurred before his first battle, when he offered an unlawful sacrifice rather than wait for Samuel (1 Samuel 13). The tactical logic was sound - his troops were deserting and the Philistines were massing - but he disobeyed the prophet's command.

More seriously, Saul failed to completely destroy the evil Amalekites as commanded, "Now go and strike down Amalek and destroy everything he has. Have no pity on him" (1 Samuel 15:2). Instead, "Saul, as well as the people, took pity on Agag" (1 Samuel 15:9) sparing the Amalekite king and the best of their livestock. This decision would have devastating consequences. God immediately appears to Samuel, saying "I have reconsidered My having made King Saul, for he has turned away from Me and has not fulfilled My word" (1 Samuel 15:11).

His third grave error revealed a disturbing moral inversion: while he had shown mercy to the Amalekite king, Saul ordered the massacre of dozens of God-fearing priests from the city of Nob, along with their families and livestock (1 Samuel 22).

Most tellingly, after the devastating capture of the Ark of the Covenant, Saul made no attempt to restore it to its proper place at the center of Israelite worship. After the Philistines returned the Ark, it remained abandoned at Kiriath-Jearim (1 Samuel 7:1), largely forgotten during Saul's entire reign. Religious and spiritual matters such as the Ark and the construction of a proper Temple were outside his primary sphere of interest. These spiritual flaws reflected the nature of Saul's mission and the stage of national development that Israel had reached.

The limitations of Saul's approach became most apparent in his relationship with David, the young shepherd who would become his son-in-law and successor. When David appeared on the scene to face Goliath, the contrast between the two leaders was immediately evident. Whereas Saul approached the Philistine threat as a military problem requiring a kinetic solution, David understood it as a spiritual challenge that could only be met through faith in God.

David's victory over Goliath was achieved not through superior weaponry or tactical brilliance, but through absolute confidence in God. "You come to me with sword and spear and javelin," David declared to the giant, "but I come to you in the name of the Lord of hosts, the God of the armies of Israel, whom you have defied" (1 Samuel 17:45).

This spiritual dimension of leadership represented the next stage of Israel's development. David understood that political independence and military strength, while necessary, were insufficient for fulfilling Israel's ultimate purpose. The nation needed not just physical security and political legitimacy, but spiritual vitality and moral authority. Saul's tragic flaw was his inability to recognize that his own successful reign had created the conditions for this next stage of development. Rather than mentoring David and preparing for a smooth transition, Saul became consumed with jealousy and spent his final years trying to eliminate the very person God had chosen to complete what he had begun.

David married Saul's daughter Michal, became best friends with Saul's son Jonathan, and won the affection of the entire people through his military exploits and charismatic leadership. Saul felt threatened and repeatedly tried to kill David, only to be outwitted time and again by the man who would become Israel's greatest king.

Saul's final days were marked by bouts of depression and rage as he lost his grip on the kingdom he had worked so hard to build. King Saul and his son Jonathan died together in battle against the Philistines on Mount Gilboa, ending a reign that had lasted approximately twenty years but whose fundamental achievements would endure forever.

Following long periods of instability and persecution under the judges, Saul had successfully answered the people's desire to have a king and to be "like all other nations." He established Israel's credibility as a regional power and created the foundation upon which his successors would build.

Despite his tragic end, King Saul is remembered positively in Jewish tradition. The rabbis understood that his failures stemmed not from evil intentions but from the burden of being first - of creating a monarchy without precedent, of making decisions no Israelite king had faced before, of building something entirely new while under constant existential threat.

Thousands of years later, this same deep psychological desire for normalization and security would once again become the primary motivation of the Jewish people following even longer periods of instability and persecution. After nearly two millennia of exile, pogroms, expulsions, and ultimately the Holocaust, the Jewish people once again yearned for the dignity and security that could only come from sovereign statehood.

The prophet Isaiah posed a rhetorical question that seemed impossible when it was written: "Can a nation be born in a day?" (Isaiah 66:8). Yet that's precisely what happened on May 14, 1948, when the State of Israel was proclaimed and immediately recognized by the world's superpowers. Jewish leaders gathered on a Friday afternoon in Tel Aviv and signed Israel's Declaration of Independence which declared "the natural right of the Jewish people to be masters of their own fate, like all other nations, in their own sovereign State," echoing the ancient Israelites' request to Samuel.

But this miraculous nation born in a day was actually the culmination of decades of patient preparation, visionary leadership, and the same kind of foundational work that King Saul had performed three millennia earlier. To understand how this ancient pattern repeated itself in modern times, we must go back to the intellectual and spiritual preparation that made modern Zionism possible. The story of the State of Israel begins not in 1948, but in the previous century.

In 1867, the American writer, Samuel Clemens, embarked on a journey that would take him through Europe and the Middle East as part of an American church group excursion. The material Clemens gathered, published under a pen name, formed the basis of *The Innocents Abroad*, the riveting travelogue that would make him one of America's most celebrated authors, known as Mark Twain.

Twain was a natural skeptic, unimpressed by religious sentimentality or romantic notions about the Holy Land. He wrote irreverently about Palestine's legendary sites, deflating the pious expectations of Christian pilgrims with wit and brutal honesty. But in doing so, Twain provided what would become crucial documentation of the land's condition just decades before the Zionist enterprise would transform it beyond recognition.

"Palestine sits in sackcloth and ashes," Twain wrote, and "over it broods the spell of a curse that has withered its fields and fettered its energies." He might not have realized it at the time, but by documenting these curses during his visit, Mark Twain provided evidence that would later support the Biblical prophecies about the land's desolation during the Jewish exile and its eventual restoration.

Throughout "The Innocents Abroad," Twain explicitly documented that the region was largely desolate and devoid of significant population. Riding on horseback through the Jezreel Valley, the famous biblical region that would soon be transformed into one of Israel's most productive agricultural areas, Twain was struck by Palestine's barren emptiness of the landscape. "There is not a solitary village throughout its whole extent," he wrote, "not for 30 miles in either direction."

It's important to understand that "Palestine" was not a country, state, or nation - it was merely an administrative designation for an Ottoman province. The name itself was chosen by the Roman Emperor Hadrian after crushing the Bar Kokhba revolt in the second century, intended as a deliberate mockery of the defeated Jews.

Following Bar Kochba's uprising, the Romans sought to weaken Jewish national identity and sever their connection to their land. They renamed Judea "Syria Palestina," invoking the Philistines - the Jewish enemy who had disappeared from history a millennium earlier. The name persisted for centuries, but it always referred to a geographic region, never to a specific people or political entity.

As the world's most famous eyewitness to the 19th century condition of the Holy Land, Twain brought global attention to the region's desolate state and inadvertently proved that Palestine was indeed "a land without a people" awaiting "a people without a land" - just a few years before that would all change forever.

INTELLECTUAL FOUNDATIONS

While Twain was documenting the physical condition of the land, Jewish thinkers across Europe were beginning to articulate the intellectual and spiritual foundations for its restoration. The Ottoman Empire, which had ruled the region for more than 500 years and controlled vast territories stretching across three continents, was showing clear signs of decline. Tsar Nicholas I of Russia had already referred to it as "The Sick Man of Europe" as early as 1853, and perceptive observers could see that the empire's days were numbered.

This period of Ottoman decline coincided with what historians call the age of nation-states. Across Europe, stateless peoples like Italians, Germans, Hungarians, and Poles were beginning to articulate visions of national self-determination based on shared history, language, culture, and territory. The idea that distinct peoples deserved their own sovereign state was taking hold and gaining momentum and would eventually reshape the entire European political map.

Among the Jewish thinkers influenced by this nationalist awakening was Rabbi Yehuda Alkalai (1798-1878), who lived in the Ottoman Empire during a time of Serbian revolts against Ottoman rule. These uprisings inspired him to think in explicitly national terms about the Jewish people's future. For decades, Alkalai served as rabbi of Zemun, a town on the Danube River directly across from Belgrade. At the time, Zemun was a relatively small Jewish community, home to Simon Herzl, who would share his rabbi's passion about Jewish nationalism with his grandson Theodor decades later.

Unlike secular nationalists, Alkalai's vision was deeply rooted in religious sources and profoundly influenced by his study of *Kabbalah* (Jewish mysticism). He believed that the physical resettlement of the Holy Land was not merely a practical necessity but a fulfillment of the biblical concept known as the Ingathering of the Exiles, and mentioned repeatedly throughout Scripture.

> "Then the Lord your God will restore your fortunes. He will have compassion on you and gather you back from all the nations where he has scattered you. Even if you have been banished to the ends of the earth, from there the Lord your God will gather you. He will bring you to the land that belonged to your ancestors, and you will possess it again." (Deuteronomy 30:3-5)

Beginning in the 1840s, Alkalai advocated for practical steps toward Jewish resettlement of Jerusalem through organized colonies and the establishment of autonomous self-governance.

More than just a solution to Jewish suffering, Alkalai understood that this restoration had universal implications and was necessary for the world's spiritual development. He taught that Jewish return to the land would hasten the messianic redemption and usher in an age of global harmony that would benefit all of humanity, an early articulation of what we are now referring to as Universal Zionism.

Across Europe, both geographically and intellectually, another pioneering thinker was developing similar ideas to Alkalai, but from a very different perspective. Moses Hess (1812-1875) was born in the French Empire into a Jewish merchant family and educated in radical German philosophy. Unlike the traditional

Rabbi Alkalai, Hess approached Jewish nationalism through the lens of contemporary European political thought.

In 1862, Hess published a groundbreaking book in German called, "Rome and Jerusalem," in which he argued that the Jews were not merely a religious community but a distinct nation whose future depended on national revival in their indigenous homeland. His analysis was remarkably prescient. Hess believed that the emergence of modern nation-states was part of God's universal plan for history, and that just as nations like France, Germany, and Italy had unique cultural and spiritual gifts to contribute to civilization, the Jewish people also had their own historic mission that could only be fulfilled through national restoration.

Hess drew a powerful parallel between two ancient cities that shaped western civilization. Rome, representing political power and imperial ambition, gave the world legal systems, administrative structures and a global religion. Jerusalem, representing ethical religion and social justice, gave the world moral law and spiritual vision. The return to Jerusalem was not just important for the Jews, it was essential for the moral development of all humanity. "The Jews will not be saved for their own sake alone," Hess wrote, "but their rebirth will uplift mankind."

Unfortunately, Hess's ideas were ahead of their time. The book sold only a few hundred copies during his lifetime and wasn't translated into other languages until 1899, two years after Herzl convened the First Zionist Congress. But the intellectual foundation Moses Hess established would prove crucial for future generations of Zionist thinkers.

While rabbis and intellectuals were developing the theoretical framework for Jewish nationalism, practical philanthropists began taking concrete steps to improve conditions for Jews already living in the Holy Land. The transition from ideas to action required resources, organization, and most importantly, individuals willing to risk their reputations and fortunes on what most contemporaries considered an impossible dream.

Moses Montefiore (1784-1885) was a wealthy British Jew who used his considerable resources and international influence to defend Jewish communities worldwide. Knighted by Queen Victoria, Sir Moses became something of an unofficial Jewish diplomat, intervening to protect Jews from blood libels and discriminatory decrees from Damascus to St. Petersburg. His wealth and connections gave him access to government officials and international leaders who would listen to his advocacy on behalf of persecuted Jewish communities.

The poverty and vulnerability of the Jews living in Palestine was particularly troubling to Montefiore. Small Jewish communities had maintained a continuous presence in the sacred cities of Jerusalem, Tiberias, Hebron, and Safed for centuries, but the "Old Yishuv" (the Old Settlement), as these ancient communities were known, was almost entirely dependent on charity from Jews abroad and had no sustainable economic base of its own. Most Jews in the Holy Land lived in dire poverty, subject to the whims of Ottoman officials and vulnerable to attacks from hostile neighbors.

Montefiore began sponsoring practical projects designed to help these poor Jews achieve economic self-sufficiency. He funded the construction of a windmill in Jerusalem in 1857 to grind flour for bread, creating local jobs and helping his brethren become less dependent on expensive imported goods. The famous Montefiore Windmill, still visible on the Jerusalem skyline today, became a symbol of the city's transition from passive charity to active development.

In 1860, Montefiore built the first Jewish neighborhood outside Jerusalem's Old City walls, demonstrating that Jews could live securely beyond the cramped confines of the Jewish Quarter. He funded agricultural schools to train young Jews in farming techniques, recognizing that the transformation of the Jewish people from a diaspora community into a normal nation would require a return to productive labor and connection with the soil.

The culmination of these early efforts came in 1878 with the founding of Petah Tikva by religious Jews from Jerusalem. Often considered the first modern Jewish agricultural settlement, Petah Tikva ("Gateway of Hope") represented a crucial transition from individual philanthropy to collective colonization. The settlers faced enormous challenges from malaria, hostile neighbors and inexperience with farming, but their success proved that large-scale Jewish agricultural settlement was possible.

The shift from proto-Zionism to full-fledged Zionist activity required a catalytic event that would convince even assimilated Jews that their future security depended on Jewish self governance. That catalyst came in the form of the Dreyfus Affair, which shattered the illusions of Jews who believed that integration into European society would solve the problem of antisemitism that had plagued the Jewish people throughout the exile, but was clearly intensifying as a result of nationalism.

In 1894, French Army Captain Alfred Dreyfus was wrongly accused of betraying his country by passing military secrets to Germany. The only "evidence" was a handwritten note discovered in a German wastebasket - later shown to be a forgery - that led to his conviction for high treason. Dreyfus, a secular Jew, soon became the target of a storm of antisemitism that shattered illusions of Jewish acceptance in modern Europe. In the very heart of Enlightenment France - a nation that prided itself on liberty, equality, and reason - Dreyfus was publicly degraded, stripped of his rank in a humiliating ceremony, while frenzied crowds shouted in the streets, "Death to the Jews!"

Witnessing this eruption of antisemitism in one of Europe's most enlightened nations convinced a young Austrian journalist that Jews urgently needed their own homeland. That journalist's response to the Dreyfus Affair would take the scattered ideas and modest efforts of earlier Jewish nationalists and shape them into a worldwide political movement that would change the course of history.

The foundation laid by the King from the tribe of Benjamin three thousand years earlier was about to find its modern parallel in the person Benjamin Netanyahu identified as his political hero - Theodor (Binyamin) Herzl, the founder of Political Zionism who would prove that, "if you will it, it is no dream."

ONCE IN THOUSANDS OF YEARS

When Theodor Herzl entered a room, conversations stopped and all heads turned. There was something magnetic about the man. His commanding height, his penetrating dark eyes, his meticulously groomed beard that gave him an almost biblical gravitas. Those who met him never forgot the encounter. One delegate to the First Zionist Congress, wrote that he was mesmerized when Herzl took the podium for he possessed a "stature, lofty as King Saul's."

But Herzl's impact went far beyond his striking appearance. Here was a man who accomplished more in just ten years of Zionist activity than most leaders achieve in a lifetime. When the Dreyfus Affair awakened his Jewish consciousness, he was thirty-four years old. When he died, exhausted by his relentless efforts to create a Jewish state, he was only forty-four. Yet in that brief span, he transformed an impossible dream into an inevitable reality.

David Ben-Gurion, who would become Israel's first prime minister, understood Herzl's unique place in history. Upon learning of Herzl's death in 1904, Ben-Gurion wrote to a friend, "Never again will there be such an extraordinary man who combines within himself the heroism of the Maccabees and the strategic genius of King David... Such a prodigy is born only once in thousands of years."

Theodor Herzl was born in 1860 in Budapest, then part of the sprawling Austro-Hungarian Empire, to Jacob and Jeanette. By all external appearances, the Herzl family represented the successful Jewish assimilation that many believed was the answer to centuries of persecution. They spoke German rather than Yiddish, celebrated Christmas alongside Jewish holidays, and moved easily in non-Jewish society.

Yet beneath this assimilated exterior, something deeper stirred in young Theodor's imagination. His paternal grandfather, Simon Herzl, had lived in Zemun, Serbia, where he was active in the local Jewish community and was deeply influenced by his rabbi, Yehuda Alkalai, mentioned earlier as one of the early advocates for Jewish return to the Land of Israel. Simon's passion for Zion left an indelible impression on his grandson. "In my youth," Herzl wrote in his diary, "I heard my grandfather speak of the Land of Israel with such fervor that it burned into my memory. He longed for Zion with all his heart."

This early exposure to the dream of Jewish restoration planted seeds that would lie dormant for decades before flowering into the most consequential political movement in modern Jewish history. But even as a child, Theodor seemed destined for something extraordinary, as revealed by a remarkable dream he experienced at age twelve, a dream so unbelievable that he kept it secret for most of his life.

Only a few months before he died, Herzl shared this childhood vision with his biographer, Reuven Brainin, who was so astonished by the account that he made sure to transcribe Herzl's words verbatim. The dream, published in Brainin's 1919 biography "The Life of Herzl," offers a glimpse into the spiritual depths of a man often dismissed as an ignorant and secular Jew:

"One night, I had a wonderful dream. The King Messiah came, and he was old and glorious. He lifted me in his arms, and he soared with me on the wings of the wind. On one of the clouds full of splendor, we encountered the figure of Moses. His appearance was like that of Moses hewn in marble by Michelangelo, for in my early childhood, I loved to look at photographs of that statue. And the Messiah called to Moses, 'For this child I have prayed!' Then he turned to me and said, 'Go and announce to the Jews that I will soon come and perform great miracles for my people and for the whole world.' I woke up, and it was only a dream. I kept this dream a secret and didn't dare tell it to anybody."

This extraordinary revelation illuminates crucial aspects of Herzl's character that would shape his future mission. Though his family was assimilated and externally secular, the twelve-year-old boy was clearly steeped in biblical imagery and Jewish messianic hopes. Even more remarkably, the dream linked Jewish redemption with universal salvation: "great miracles for my people and for the whole world."

The young Herzl's intuitive understanding that Jewish restoration would bless all of mankind represents another early glimpse of Universal Zionism, the recognition that Israel's success is not only for the Jews, but is the key to unlocking unprecedented blessings for all nations.

As Herzl matured, he seemed to move further away from his Jewish roots. He became a successful journalist and playwright, moving in sophisticated European circles where Jewish identity was considered an embarrassing relic of the medieval past. His plays were performed in leading theaters, his articles appeared in prestigious publications, and his lifestyle reflected the cultural sophistication of Vienna.

Yet even during his most assimilated period, Herzl remained troubled by the persistence of antisemitism. He was particularly disturbed by the way Jew hatred was intensifying rather than diminishing as Jews became more integrated into European society. The promise of the Enlightenment, that reason and education would eliminate prejudice, was proving false, and Herzl began searching for more radical solutions.

In 1893, a full year before the Dreyfus Affair would transform his worldview, Herzl conceived an audacious plan that revealed both his desperation and his willingness to think outside conventional boundaries. He proposed arranging a meeting with Pope Leo XIII to enlist papal support in the struggle against antisemitism. In exchange for the Church's protection, Herzl proposed the mass conversion of Jewish children to Christianity in a grand public ceremony at St. Stephen's Cathedral in Vienna.

"I would like to call upon all Jews to meet in broad daylight, at noon on a Sunday, in front of St. Stephen's Cathedral," he wrote in his diary. "We would march there proudly, and then the church bells would ring. Not in shame, as individuals have converted up to now, but with proud gestures... Then the conversion would be complete. The leaders would remain Jewish, but they would have made it possible for their children to merge with Christians through an honest manner."

This startling suggestion reveals the depth of Herzl's despair about Jewish prospects in Europe, but also his fundamental misunderstanding of antisemitism's true nature. He still believed that the Jewish problem was essentially one of religious differences that could be solved through elimination of that distinction. He had not yet grasped that modern antisemitism was not a problem for Christians to solve, but a signal for Jews to transform their own behavior and worldview.

Everything changed with the outbreak of the Dreyfus Affair in 1894. Covering the trial as a correspondent for the *Neue Freie Presse*, Herzl witnessed something that shattered his assumptions about Jewish integration in Europe. Here was Alfred Dreyfus, a French army officer, a patriot who had devoted his life to serving his country, a man who embodied everything that Jewish assimilationists aspired to become. Yet when he was falsely accused of treason, the crowds in the Paris streets screamed not "Death to the traitor!" but "Death to the Jews!"

At that moment, Herzl experienced a revelation. If antisemitism could explode with such venom in France, the birthplace of the Declaration of the Rights of Man, the nation that was the first to grant full citizenship to the Jews, then no level of assimilation, or Jewish contributions to society, would ever provide long term safety and security.

The idea that struck him with the force of divine inspiration seemed just as radical as his mass conversion proposal, but pointed in the exact opposite direction. Instead of dissolving the Jewish people into the surrounding population, why not restore them to their own land where they could build their own society?

What transformed Herzl from an isolated dreamer into the founder of a world changing movement was his remarkable ability to combine visionary imagination with practical organization. Within months of his Dreyfus awakening, he wrote *Der Judenstaat* (The Jewish State), a political manifesto that laid out in detail how a modern Jewish state could be created through diplomacy, finance, and mass migration.

Just weeks after *The Jewish State* appeared in bookstores, an early reader picked up a copy and immediately went to track down the author. Reverend William Hechler, the Anglican chaplain of the British Embassy in Vienna, read it with growing excitement. Unlike most of his Jewish contemporaries who dismissed Herzl's ideas as fantasy, Hechler recognized something prophetic in the young journalist's vision.

Hechler believed that the Jews' return to the Land of Israel was not merely a political possibility but a biblical inevitability, foretold in Scripture and essential to God's plan. As a student of biblical prophecy, he had been watching for signs that this restoration was approaching. On March 10, 1896, Hechler appeared unannounced at Herzl's apartment, clutching a copy of *The Jewish State* under his arm.

"Here I am," said Hechler, standing in Herzl's doorway.

"That I can see," replied Herzl, "but who are you?"

"You are puzzled," Hechler observed. "But you see, as long ago as 1882, I predicted your arrival... Now I am going to help you."

This dramatic encounter represents the first recorded meeting between Jewish Zionism and Christian Zionism, a match made in heaven. Herzl was initially skeptical of this enthusiastic clergyman, but was quickly won over by Hechler's vast biblical knowledge, his genuine love for the Jewish people, and most importantly, his impressive political connections. Here was a man who not only understood Herzl's vision but possessed the access to European high society that Herzl desperately needed.

Hechler became Herzl's guide through the labyrinthine world of European diplomacy, opening doors that would have otherwise remained permanently closed. Hechler introduced Herzl to members of the German royal family, including Grand Duke Friedrich I of Baden, who in turn facilitated Herzl's meetings with Kaiser Wilhelm II. This partnership between the Jewish visionary and the Christian chaplain established a pattern that would define the Zionist movement: the recognition that Jewish restoration was not merely a Jewish interest but a spiritual imperative that transcended religious boundaries.

While Reverend Hechler embraced Herzl's vision with evangelical fervor, the response from established Jewish religious leadership was dramatically different. When Herzl sought support from the rabbinic authorities who should have been his natural allies, he encountered nearly universal opposition from the Jewish world.

REFORM REJECTION & ORTHODOX OPPOSITION

Herzl first approached the Reform rabbis he felt most comfortable with. However, the Reform movement, which had emerged in 19th-century Germany as Judaism's attempt to integrate with European society, viewed Herzl's nationalism as a dangerous step backward.

Reform rabbis saw Herzl's call for a separate Jewish state as not only unnecessary but counterproductive. If Jews were finally being accepted as equals in civilized society, why would they voluntarily segregate themselves in some distant Oriental backwater? Political Zionism seemed to validate the antisemitic charge that Jews could never be loyal citizens of their host countries.

For decades, Reform leaders had argued that Judaism was purely a religious faith, not a national identity, and that Jews could be fully German, French, or American while maintaining their religious distinctiveness. For Reform Judaism, the emancipation of European Jewry represented the true fulfillment of messianic prophecy. They found their promised land in the civil liberties granted by enlightened European governments. Abraham Geiger, a founding father of Reform Judaism, captured this sentiment when he declared, "Berlin is our Jerusalem!" His American counterparts were equally emphatic: "America is our Zion!" they proclaimed, seeing the United States as the ultimate realization of Jewish hopes for equality and prosperity.

Orthodox Jewish opposition to Herzl came from the opposite direction but was equally vehement. While Reform Judaism rejected Zionism for being too particularistic, Orthodox leadership condemned it for being too secular. How could the sacred return to the Holy Land be led by a non-observant, assimilated Jew like Theodor Herzl?

Many Orthodox rabbis taught that the Jewish exile was a divine punishment that would only end through divine intervention. Human beings must not attempt to force God's hand through political action. The Ingathering of the Exiles promised in Torah prophecy would only occur when God chose to send the Messiah, who would return the Jewish people to their land miraculously "on the wings of eagles" - not through steamships and railway cars.

Moreover, Orthodox leaders were deeply suspicious of Herzl's secular vision for the Jewish state. What kind of Jewish society would emerge from a movement led by a man who violated the Sabbath, ate non-kosher food, and seemed more interested in European culture than Jewish tradition? Better to wait for God's own redemption than to participate in what appeared to be a godless nationalist enterprise.

The depth of religious opposition to Herzl became clear when Reform and Orthodox leaders, bitter rivals who agreed on virtually nothing else, joined forces to oppose Political Zionism. These two movements, which had been engaged in theological warfare for decades, found common ground in their shared conviction that Herzl's nationalism posed a threat to their respective visions of Jewish destiny. Together, they issued a joint statement published at first in the name of the German Rabbinical Association and then republished in English in the influential London-based *Jewish Chronicle* in July 1897, condemning the Zionist movement: "The endeavors of the so-called Zionists to found a Jewish national state in Palestine runs counter to the messianic prophecies of Judaism," they wrote.

This religious coalition against Zionism created immediate practical problems for Herzl's organizing efforts. When he announced plans to convene the first World Zionist Congress in Munich, centrally located for European Jewish communities, local rabbinic leaders, both Reform and Orthodox, pressured city authorities to deny permits for the gathering.

Reform and Orthodox rabbis warned that hosting a Zionist conference would create public disturbances and make German Jews appear disloyal to their fatherland. Faced with this religious opposition in Germany, Herzl was forced to hastily relocate his congress to Switzerland, where he would be less vulnerable to organized Jewish resistance.

After the publication of *The Jewish State*, Herzl embarked on a speaking tour across Europe, carrying his revolutionary message to Jewish communities across the continent. The response revealed a stark divide that would define the Zionist movement up to the present day. Writing to a colleague in frustration, Herzl captured the paradox he encountered everywhere: "The Jews today have no more burning aspiration than to be invisible among the nations... They are more English than the English, more French than the French, more German than the Germans. Only the Zionists, my friends, want to be Jewish Jews."

Nevertheless, Herzl remained undeterred. If the Jewish establishment was not willing to take political action for their persecuted brethren, then new leadership would have to emerge from the grassroots.

While the comfortable middle class and the elite establishment viewed Herzl's nationalism as an embarrassing development, the masses were eager for a savior. Among the poor, uneducated Eastern European Jews suffering under religious oppression, Herzl's message ignited hope like a spark in dry tinder. Here was a secular messiah offering not just escape from persecution, but dignity, sovereignty, and a future their children could build with their own hands.

HERZL GOES TO BASEL

When the First Zionist Congress convened at the Basel Stadtcasino concert hall in August 1897, delegates arrived from across Europe and as far away as Palestine and the United States. Herzl wanted this gathering to be remembered for posterity, and he staged it accordingly. The Congress opened with pageantry designed to proclaim Jewish dignity to the world, both to inspire the delegates themselves and to command respect from foreign observers watching this unprecedented assembly of Jews.

With the theatrical flair of a master showman, Herzl transformed what could have been a modest meeting into something approaching a national parliament in exile. Every detail was carefully orchestrated to project seriousness and statesmanship. He insisted that all delegates wear formal attire, not the traditional garb that marked Jews as different, but the same elegant clothing worn by parliamentarians and diplomats throughout Europe.

Herzl himself appeared in a formal black frock coat, white tie, and gloves, carrying himself as a head of state. When he noticed that his close associate Max Nordau had arrived in ordinary clothing, Herzl insisted that Nordau return to his hotel and change into a tuxedo and top hat. Only Rabbi Shmuel Mohliver was permitted to wear traditional rabbinic garb, and only because he didn't own a tuxedo! The message conveyed through every carefully chosen detail at the First Zionist Congress was unmistakable. The Jewish people are a nation like other nations, deserving of the same respect and recognition.

The first Congress achieved far more than symbolic significance. Over the course of three days, the 204 delegates debated and voted on institutions that remain central to the Zionist movement today. They adopted the blue and white flag whose pattern echoed the Jewish prayer shawl. They selected the recently written *Hatikvah* (The Hope) as their anthem, its stirring melody carrying words that had sustained the Jews for centuries: "Our hope is not yet lost, the hope of two thousand years, to be a free nation in our land, the land of Zion and Jerusalem."

More practically, they created the Jewish National Fund to systematically acquire territory in Palestine through coordinated fundraising efforts. They formalized the World Zionist Organization as the umbrella institution that would coordinate activities across national boundaries and ideological differences.

Most importantly, they articulated the Basel Program, a clear, achievable political agenda that would guide the movement for the next half-century. The Basel Program established that, "Zionism seeks to establish a home for the Jewish people in Palestine secured under public law." This careful formulation balanced idealistic vision with diplomatic realism, avoiding inflammatory language that would further antagonize the anti-Zionists while establishing an unmistakable goal.

Considering the centuries of animosity between Christians and Jews, among the most remarkable aspects of the First Zionist Congress was the official presence of ten non-Jews, whose participation demonstrated that Herzl's vision had begun to transcend traditional boundaries. While Jewish leadership remained trapped in debates about Jewish identity and the wisdom of nationalistic advocacy, a new alliance was forming between Jewish visionaries and Christian supporters who recognized biblical prophecy unfolding.

The most distinguished of these Christian participants was Henry Dunant. A Swiss humanitarian, Dunant's traumatic experience witnessing battlefield carnage in Italy had led him to establish the International Red Cross and draft the Geneva Convention. For these efforts, Dunant would receive the first Nobel Peace Prize in 1901. Yet decades earlier, well before Basel, Dunant had already taken up another cause: advocating for the Jewish return to

Palestine through an organization he founded, the International Society for the Renewal of the Orient.

When Dunant met Herzl, the Zionist leader was struck by the humanitarian's passionate commitment to Jewish nationalism. In his correspondence, Herzl referred to Dunant as a "Christian Zionist", the first recorded use of that term, marking the beginning of a movement that would prove crucial to Israel's eventual success.

Reverend William Hechler also attended as Herzl's honored guest. For his passionate advocacy on behalf of the fledgling movement, Hechler received not only an invitation to the Congress but a lifetime pension from the World Zionist Organization, support that continued until his death in 1931.

The participation of these Christian Zionists provided something invaluable that Jewish nationalism alone could never achieve: legitimacy in the eyes of Christian Europe. Here were respected Christian leaders affirming that Jewish restoration was not merely an ethnic aspiration but a moral imperative rooted in divine promise and historical justice.

On the final evening of the Congress, alone in his Basel hotel room, Herzl wrote in his diary:

> "Were I to sum up the Basel Congress in a word, which I shall guard against pronouncing publicly, it would be this: At Basel I founded the Jewish State. If I said this out loud today, I would be greeted by universal laughter. In five years perhaps, and certainly in fifty years, everyone will perceive it."

These words, penned exactly fifty years and nine months before David Ben-Gurion proclaimed Israel's independence, showcase the visionary clarity that set Herzl apart. At the First Zionist Congress, the Jewish State was not yet created in land or population, but in something more enduring - a vision. Upon that vision, everything that followed would rest: the diplomacy, the settlements, the battles, the recognition of nations. All of it traced back to the foundation laid in a Swiss concert hall over three remarkable days in August 1897.

What distinguished Herzl from other nationalists of his era was his understanding that Jewish restoration would benefit not only Jews. Unlike the narrow tribal nationalism that was reshaping Europe, Herzl's Zionism contained within it the seeds of universal redemption.

A man of letters, Herzl used another, more creative, form of writing to convey his ideas. In 1902, he wrote a novel called *Altneuland*, in which he envisioned the Jewish state in utopian terms, as a beacon of progress that would inspire social and technological advancement throughout the world. His fictional Palestine was a model society that eliminated poverty, achieved equality between different ethnic and religious groups, and pioneered innovations in agriculture, industry, and governance that other nations would eagerly adopt.

In retrospect, Herzl would indeed deserve Ben-Gurion's description of him as a once-in-a-thousand-years Jewish hero. Yet in his own time, he was met with fierce opposition. Jewish critics are nothing new; even Moses, our greatest teacher, faced relentless detractors. The Bible recounts how Korach led a rebellion against the very authority of Moses - challenging the greatest prophet in Jewish history at the very height of his mission.

Similarly, the Scroll of Esther, after recounting Mordechai's astonishing achievements, adds a striking detail almost in passing. Having just saved the Jews of Persia from annihilation, the Book concludes: "Mordechai was respected by most of his brethren." Most, but not all. From our earliest history, the precedent was set: *two Jews, three opinions.* Herzl was no exception to this eternal pattern.

Reform and ultra-Orthodox leaders continued their attacks on Zionism from the outside, while internal voices within the movement itself began to grumble, questioning Herzl's methods and priorities. The very success of the Zionist Congress unleashed forces that Herzl struggled to control.

From the outset, the influential Jewish essayist Asher Ginsberg who wrote under the pen name Ahad Ha'am ("One of the People" in Hebrew) argued that Herzl's single-minded drive for immediate political action was both premature and misguided. Born in the Russian Empire, Ahad Ha'am (1856–1927) emerged as the leading voice of "Cultural Zionism" and became the most widely read Hebrew writer of his time. Herzl, by contrast, wrote and spoke in German; though he admired Hebrew, he regarded its revival as secondary to his political aims.

When it came to Zionism, Ahad Ha'am advocated for cultural advancement first, followed only later by political efforts. He dismissed Herzl's timeline as completely unrealistic, writing, "Only a fantasy bordering on madness can believe that as soon as the Jewish State is established, millions of Jews will flock to it, and the land will afford them adequate sustenance. We must confess to ourselves that the 'ingathering of the exiles' is unattainable by natural means." Ahad Ha'am's ideological debate with Herzl was fierce, and many of their arguments echo still today.

The accusations of "madness" from his various opponents became so frequent that Herzl complained about it to one of his closest colleagues, Max Nordau, a psychologist. Nordau's reply to Herzl became legendary in Zionist circles, "If you are mad, then I am mad as well. I'm behind you, and you can count on me!"

Yet dissent continued to grow within the movement. After the first Congress, delegates began splintering into distinct camps, each with its own vision of Jewish restoration. Herzl led the Political Zionists and Ahad Ha'am commanded the Cultural Zionists. In addition, Ze'ev Jabotinsky emerged as the leader of

Revisionist Zionism, which advocated for a more militaristic response, while Rabbi Samuel Mohilver represented the Religious Zionists, insisting that any return to the land must be grounded in traditional Jewish law and values.

These diverse camps engaged in heated debates over the future of Zionism, and as in any true democracy, the clash of ideas only sharpened them further. Like Judaism itself, the diversity within the Zionist movement was not a liability to be endured but a strength to be cultivated. Their spirited exchanges brought essential perspectives to the table, shaping fundamental questions that continue to resonate to this day.

At the time, these debates were not only vigorous but often fierce and personal, threatening the fragile coalition Herzl had so carefully built. Nowhere was the danger greater than at the Sixth Zionist Congress in 1903, during the emotional confrontation over the "Uganda Proposal." Sparked in the wake of brutal pogroms against Russian Jews, the crisis laid bare a clash between desperate urgency and uncompromising principle - a tension that would shape Zionist politics for generations to come.

THE UGANDA CRISIS

On Easter Sunday of 1903, disaster struck the Jewish world with devastating force and far reaching consequences. Stirred up by Christian antisemitism in church on their holy day, Russian peasants attacked their Jewish neighbors in the city of Kishinev. The town had a population of about 100,000 Russians, half of whom were Jewish who had been living there for close to a century. In scenes that would tragically foreshadow October 7th more than a century later, dozens of Jews were murdered, hundreds wounded, women raped, and more than 1,000 Jewish homes, synagogues and businesses were destroyed over a period of two days.

The brutal pogrom shocked the world. Like the Dreyfus Affair in the previous decade, international press coverage of Kishinev awakened global consciousness about the precarious situation of European Jewry and convinced many Zionists that immediate refuge was desperately needed. Following the massacre, world powers demonstrated sympathy for the Jews. Many speeches were given in parliaments decrying the violence and British Colonial Secretary Joseph Chamberlain responded by making Herzl a controversial proposal.

England offered 15,000 square kilometers in East Africa, along the shores of Lake Victoria in what was then Uganda for a Jewish autonomous colony. The British saw a chance to provide humanitarian assistance while tapping into Jewish desperation and resourcefulness. They hoped to kill two birds with one tragedy, and develop an underutilized territory within their growing empire.

Traumatized by Kishinev, the ever pragmatic Herzl brought the Uganda proposal before the Sixth Zionist Congress in August 1903. He carefully framed it as a temporary refuge, a *Nachtasyl* (night shelter), that would provide safety and security while the movement continued working toward its ultimate goal in Palestine.

Though Ahad Ha'am himself wasn't a delegate at the sixth Congress, his influence was present through his disciple, a young scientist named Chaim Weizmann. The future first president of the State of Israel, Weizmann (1874-1952) considered the Uganda Plan an outrageous abandonment of Zionist values and a dangerous diversion that would misdirect Jews away from their true national revival in Palestine. He was especially critical of Herzl, whom he sharply accused of sacrificing the Zionist movement's long-term cultural mission for short-term political expediency.

When Herzl presented the Uganda Plan for a vote, the Congress erupted in emotionally charged debates. After hours of heated discussions, the final tally was decisive yet deeply divisive. 295 delegates voted in favor of the Uganda Plan, 178 against, with 98 abstentions, a count that revealed fundamental divisions about the nature and purpose of Zionism itself. Herzl quickly promised that a commission of inquiry would be sent to spy out the land, like the scouts Moses had fatefully dispatched before entering Israel.

The aftermath was heartbreaking. Many delegates, particularly those from Russia who had expected unwavering commitment to Palestine, stormed out of the hall in tears after the vote was announced. News of the dramatic episode within the nascent Zionist movement reverberated around the world in American and European newspapers, as both Jews and Christians followed developments with intense interest.

Among those closely monitoring the Uganda crisis was William Blackstone, a leading American advocate for the Jewish people in Protestant evangelical networks. Since 1890, when he had organized a conference on Zionism in his hometown of Chicago, Blackstone had been a passionate supporter of Jewish return to Palestine. In 1891, he presented the Blackstone Memorial to President Benjamin Harrison, urging the U.S. government to support Jewish restoration in their ancestral homeland.

The Blackstone Memorial was signed by over 400 prominent Americans, including business leaders like John D. Rockefeller and J.P. Morgan, members of Congress, university presidents, and Christian clergy. It framed Jewish return to the Land of Israel as both a biblical imperative and a humanitarian response to persecution and was one of the earliest American political endorsements of Zionism.

When Blackstone learned that the Zionist Congress had voted in favor of accepting territory in Africa, he was astonished. After thousands of years of exile, God was finally bringing His Chosen People back to their Promised Land, and they had voted on a detour to Uganda? The American pastor couldn't believe what he was hearing and he did what any faithful Christian might do. Blackstone grabbed a Bible from his shelf, underlined all the passages referring to the divine promise of the return to Israel, and sent the marked-up copy directly to Herzl. Blackstone's point was unmistakable. The promises of God were clear and eternal, and no human vote could alter the divine decree that had designated Palestine as the Jewish homeland!

The Uganda debate had taken its toll on Herzl, who was physically exhausted by the ensuing turmoil. The Blackstone Bible made its way across the Atlantic to Herzl's desk in Vienna, reminding the embattled leader that Zionism wasn't just for Jews, but served an important role for Christians as well. The book was by his bedside when Herzl's heart gave out, just months after the divisive Uganda debate had nearly torn apart the movement he had worked so tirelessly to build.

Theodor Herzl died on July 3, 1904, at the age of forty-four, his body worn out by the relentless stress, travel, and emotional strain of fighting for the Zionist movement on multiple fronts simultaneously. The man who had transformed his naive dream into an unstoppable reality had literally given his life for the vision he had first imagined just a decade earlier.

Yet even in death, Herzl's prophecy from Basel continued to unfold. The Uganda crisis, which had seemed like it might destroy Zionism, actually strengthened the movement by clarifying its essential mission. The emotional response of the delegates had demonstrated that Palestine was not merely one option among many, but the irreplaceable center of Jewish hopes and dreams. No amount of pragmatic calculation could substitute for the spiritual connection between the Jewish people and their ancestral homeland, and the plan was formally rejected at the Seventh Zionist Congress in 1905.

The Blackstone Bible by Herzl's bedside served as an enduring symbol of the alliance between Christians and Jews that would prove crucial to Israel's restoration. While critics from the Jewish establishment had tried to stop Herzl, Christian supporters like Hechler and Blackstone had recognized the biblical significance of what was unfolding and had offered their vital encouragement at the moment when it was most needed.

Following Herzl's death, Zionism evolved from a small ideological project into an internationally recognized national movement. What followed were decades of systematic nation-building that would transform both the physical landscape of Palestine and the political map of the Middle East.

The annual Zionist Congresses became the parliament of a people in exile, coordinating efforts across continents and ideologies. The Jewish National Fund distributed blue and white collection boxes to homes around the world. In tenements from Warsaw to New York City, poor Jewish families kept these tin boxes in places of honor, contributing every spare ruble and penny toward acquiring territory in Palestine from largely absentee Arab landlords who had never even seen the remote and barren properties they owned.

Political Zionists used their newly acquired land strategically, establishing pioneering communities that would become symbols of Jewish renewal. In 1909, they founded Degania, the first kibbutz, a collective settlement where settlers shared equally in both labor and rewards. That same year witnessed an even more ambitious achievement, the establishment of the first all-Jewish city in modern history.

Built on sand dunes just north of the ancient port city of Jaffa, Tel Aviv was named after the Hebrew translation of Herzl's novel

Altneuland (Old-New Land). In Hebrew, "Tel Aviv" combines two meaningful words: *tel*, referring to an ancient mound built up from layers of ruins, and *aviv*, meaning spring or renewal. Together, the name captures the essence of the Zionist project - building something new upon old foundations. The choice reflected the settlers' deep sense of historical mission as they were not just building new communities but fulfilling venerable prophecies of national rebirth. Other settlements bore similarly symbolic names: Petah Tikva (The Door of Hope), Rishon LeZion (First in Zion), each name connecting present progress with the prophetic vision of Israel's future restoration.

The original 60 families drawing lots for plots of land on which to build the new town of Tel Aviv (Photo by Avraham Soskin, April 1909)

In addition to establishing settlements, the Zionists facilitated large-scale immigration, known in Hebrew as "Aliyah," literally meaning "to go up" and signifying the Jewish attachment of ascending to the Holy Land. Between 1904 and 1914, approximately 35,000 Jews ascended, mostly from Eastern Europe, Russia, and Poland, doubling Palestine's Jewish population and establishing a firm Jewish majority in key regions.

Unlike earlier immigrants who often relied on charity, pioneers from this wave of immigration, known as the "Second Aliyah," were determined to transform both themselves and the land through physical labor and establishing collective settlements. (The "First Aliyah" had brought approximately 25,000 Jews to Palestine, many fleeing Russian pogroms from 1882 to 1903.)

Like Herzl himself, many early Zionist leaders possessed a zeal and fervor that could only be described as biblical in intensity. Perhaps no figure embodied this more completely than Eliezer Ben-Yehuda (1858-1922), who almost single-handedly revived Hebrew as a modern spoken language after nearly two millennia of its use being limited primarily to prayer and religious study.

Born in Lithuania as Eliezer Yitzhak Perlman, he became convinced that the revival of the nation of Israel required the revival of the language of Israel. Making aliyah in 1881, Ben-Yehuda implemented his radical conviction with unwavering determination. Supported by his wife Devorah in his linguistic efforts, and later by her sister Hemda whom he married after Devorah's death, Ben-Yehuda embarked on an unprecedented experiment.

He raised his son, Itamar, as the first exclusively Hebrew speaker in modern times, strictly enforcing a Hebrew-only policy in his home despite the fact that there were virtually no other Hebrew speakers around. When young Itamar needed words for modern concepts that didn't exist in biblical Hebrew, his father would consult Scripture for inspiration or simply invent new terms on the spot.

The result was both touching and comical. Visitors and family members often had no idea what the child was saying, as Itamar chattered away in a language that existed nowhere else except in the Ben-Yehuda household. The extraordinary father was literally creating a living language in real-time, using his own son as both laboratory and test subject for one of history's most ambitious acts of cultural resurrection. Ben-Yehuda's achievements were supernatural. He developed thousands of new Hebrew words for modern concepts, compiled a massive dictionary, published Hebrew newspapers, and established the Hebrew Language Council to study his pursuit more scientifically.

*Eliezer and Hemda Ben-Yehuda, in their house in the Talpiot
neighborhood of Jerusalem (Photo by Yaakov Ben Dov)*

Through his life's work, Eliezer Ben-Yehuda transformed Hebrew from an archaic sacred language into a practical everyday vernacular capable of expressing all aspects of modern life. The rebirth of Hebrew became foundational to Israeli national identity and essential to the revival of Jewish sovereignty in the ancestral homeland.

However, while pioneering Jews in Palestine were busy building settlements and reviving a language, the foundations of the world around them were beginning to crack.

THE WINDS OF WORLD WAR

For nearly five centuries, the Ottoman Empire had been an Islamic state ruled by the Sultan-Caliph, who served as both the political and religious leader of the Muslim world. Islamic law and tradition deeply influenced the Empire's administration, legal system, and worldview, shaping its approach toward Zionism. While Islam technically recognized Jews as "People of the Book" and granted them protected status, this came with severe limitations. Jews lived as *dhimmis*, tolerated but persecuted second-class minorities subject to special taxes, legal restrictions, and social humiliation designed to reinforce their subordinate status. When the Zionist movement emerged in the late 19th century, Ottoman authorities viewed it with deep suspicion and outright hostility.

The Empire frequently took steps to limit or suppress Zionist activity, seeing organized Jewish immigration as a potential threat to Ottoman sovereignty and Islamic dominance in the region. They issued restrictive decrees limiting the number of Jews who could immigrate to Palestine from Russia and Eastern Europe, where persecution was driving mass Jewish exodus. Under the Sharia-based Ottoman legal system, land ownership by non-Muslims was severely restricted and viewed as both politically dangerous and religiously problematic.

Ottoman resistance to Jewish national revival would prove to be a fatal miscalculation. World War I erupted in 1914 following the assassination of Archduke Franz Ferdinand in Sarajevo, which triggered a catastrophic chain reaction of alliances and rivalries that drew Europe's major powers into global conflict. The Ottoman Empire's fateful decision to join Germany and Austria-Hungary would seal its doom, as it found itself fighting for its very existence against the British Empire at the height of its power. By the war's end, this strategic alignment would prove transformative. Palestine would transfer from Muslim Ottoman control to Christian British mandate, setting the stage for the eventual establishment of Jewish sovereignty. Those who had supported the Zionists found themselves on the winning side of history, while the Ottoman Empire, which had opposed Jewish restoration, joined the dustbin of fallen empires.

Zionists, both in Europe and Palestine, sided decisively with the Allies, seeing the war as their chance to help defeat the Ottomans while gaining crucial support for their national aspirations. Jewish contributions to the Allied war effort would take multiple forms, demonstrating loyalty, patriotism and capability while advancing Zionist political goals.

In England, Chaim Weizmann, who had emerged as a leading figure in the Zionist movement following Herzl's death, played a crucial role in the war effort. A brilliant chemist who had studied in Germany and Switzerland before settling in Manchester, Weizmann was conducting research when the war created an urgent crisis for the British military.

Weizmann discovered an ingenious bacterial method to produce acetone, a crucial ingredient in the explosives used by British artillery and naval forces. Prior to his breakthrough, acetone was primarily obtained from wood distillation, a process that couldn't keep pace with wartime demand. Britain was running critically short of acetone, and without a new source, military leaders warned they would lose the war within months as their ammunition supplies dwindled.

Weizmann's discovery revolutionized industrial chemistry and earned him significant influence with officials in the highest levels of the British government. His scientific contribution opened doors with key figures like Alfred Balfour and Winston Churchill that would prove invaluable as the war drew to a close.

Simultaneously, Jewish military efforts emerged as another powerful form of Zionist participation in World War I.

Ze'ev Jabotinsky (1880-1940), a fierce advocate for Jewish self-defense, had long argued that the Jewish people could never achieve true security without developing their own military capabilities. When WWI erupted, he saw a unique opportunity to prove Jewish martial valor on the world stage. In 1917, Jabotinsky co-founded the Jewish Legion alongside Lieutenant Colonel John Henry Patterson, serving as part of the British Army in order to liberate the Palestine from Ottoman rule. Patterson was a passionate supporter of Jewish nationalism who brought to the Zionist movement military expertise and credibility. An Irish Christian who had gained fame hunting man-eating lions in Kenya, Patterson served with distinction in the British Army across multiple campaigns.

The formation of the Jewish Legion was a remarkable achievement. For the first time since the destruction of the Second Temple, Jews were officially organized as a military unit fighting under a Jewish flag for explicitly Jewish national goals. More than 5,000 Jewish volunteers from Britain, America, and Palestine itself served in various battalions, participating in the liberation of their ancestral homeland from Ottoman rule.

Patterson and Jabotinsky believed that Jewish participation in the Allied war effort would not only contribute to the defeat of the Ottomans but also demonstrate that the Jews were ready for national sovereignty and capable of defending themselves. The Jewish Legion's service in the Palestinian campaign on behalf of the Allies helped lay the groundwork, both ideologically and practically, for a future Jewish army. The Legion reflected Jabotinsky's broader understanding of the need for what he called an "Iron Wall" of Jewish military strength to defend against increasingly violent local opposition.

Jabotinsky would later refer to Patterson as the "godfather of the Israeli army," recognizing how this Irish officer's support had been crucial in establishing the precedent for Jewish fighting forces. Although Patterson's name is not widely known today, his legacy lives on. John was the namesake of Israeli hero Yoni Netanyahu, Benjamin's older brother, who was the only IDF soldier to fall in the Uganda hostage rescue operation in 1976. The Netanyahu family's appreciation for Christian Zionists runs deep.

Within the Ottoman-controlled territories, military resistance to Turkish rule took other dramatic forms that revealed the depth of Jewish commitment to Allied victory. Sarah Aaronson (1890-1917), a young woman living in the newly formed town of Zikhron Yaakov, had witnessed firsthand the brutality of Ottoman rule and the suffering it inflicted on Jews in Palestine.

Aaronson established an intelligence network on behalf of the British that worked with Allied forces to provide crucial information about Ottoman military activities and troop movements. Her network included her brother Aaron, a renowned agronomist who had traveled extensively throughout the region and possessed intimate knowledge of Ottoman defenses, as well as other Jewish settlers who were willing to risk their lives for the Allied cause.

Operating under extreme personal risk, Aaronson's network, known by the acronym NILI (based on the biblical verse in 1 Samuel 15.29, "The Eternal One of Israel will not lie"), provided intelligence that significantly weakened Ottoman defenses. The information they gathered about troop positions, supply lines, and fortifications proved invaluable to British military planners and contributed to their eventual control over Palestine.

When Ottoman authorities discovered the spy ring through torture of captured operatives, Aaronson was arrested and brutally interrogated. Rather than betray her colleagues, she chose to take her own life, becoming one of the first martyrs of the

Zionist cause. Aaronson's courage and sacrifice demonstrated how the war was transforming Zionism from a primarily diplomatic and settlement-building movement into a national liberation struggle where Jews were willing to fight and die for their national aspirations.

Meanwhile, the broader British campaign in Palestine was unfolding with dramatic success. Protecting the Suez Canal, which Britain had purchased in 1875 and which served as the crucial link between England and India, became one of Britain's primary strategic objectives when war erupted. To secure this vital waterway against Ottoman and German threats, England found itself sending an army to the Holy Land for the first time in 700 years, since Richard the Lionheart's Crusaders had been driven from Jerusalem by Saladin's Muslim forces.

The British Palestinian campaign began with a series of stunning victories in the Holy Land that captured the imagination of the Christian world. In October 1917, General Edmund Allenby captured Beersheba from the Ottomans through a daring cavalry charge by Australian Light Horse units that became legendary in military history. The sight of mounted soldiers thundering across the desert towards ancient biblical cities stirred romantic and religious sentiments throughout the British Empire. With his forces now within striking distance of Jerusalem, Allenby hoped to deliver the sacred city as a Christmas present to the British people before the end of the year. The symbolic value of such a victory was not lost on British leadership, who understood that liberating Jerusalem would provide a powerful morale boost to war-weary populations across Christian Allied nations.

When Allenby did finally capture Jerusalem in December 1917, understanding the profound religious significance of his role, he dismounted his horse and walked through the Jaffa Gate on foot. He explained his gesture as a sign of respect, acknowledging that only the Messiah should enter Jerusalem riding on an animal. The symbolism was lost on no one. For the first time since the Crusades, Christian forces had liberated Jerusalem from Muslim rule, and they were about to return it to the Jews.

It was during those crucial weeks, precisely forty days between the Battle of Beersheba and the capture of Jerusalem, that Britain issued a statement that would fulfill the political aspirations that Herzl had articulated just twenty years earlier. The timing seemed divinely orchestrated, as if the liberation of the holy city had created the perfect moment for the greatest diplomatic breakthrough in Zionist history.

BALFOUR'S DECLARATION

Having worked closely with Chaim Weizmann throughout the war, British Foreign Secretary Arthur Balfour recognized the strategic value of Jewish support and the moral justice of Zionist aspirations. On November 2, 1917, Balfour sent an official letter to Lord Rothschild, head of the British Zionist Federation, containing words that would echo through history:

> "His Majesty's Government view with favour the establishment in Palestine of a national home for the Jewish people, and will use their best endeavours to facilitate the achievement of this object, it being clearly understood that nothing shall be done which may prejudice the civil and religious rights of existing non-Jewish communities in Palestine, or the rights and political status enjoyed by Jews in any other country."

Foreign Office,
November 2nd, 1917.

Dear Lord Rothschild,

I have much pleasure in conveying to you, on behalf of His Majesty's Government, the following declaration of sympathy with Jewish Zionist aspirations which has been submitted to, and approved by, the Cabinet

"His Majesty's Government view with favour the establishment in Palestine of a national home for the Jewish people, and will use their best endeavours to facilitate the achievement of this object, it being clearly understood that nothing shall be done which may prejudice the civil and religious rights of existing non-Jewish communities in Palestine, or the rights and political status enjoyed by Jews in any other country"

I should be grateful if you would bring this declaration to the knowledge of the Zionist Federation.

The Balfour Declaration issued on November 2, 1917 to Lord Walter Rothschild.

This document, known as the Balfour Declaration, represented the first time a major world power had officially endorsed Jewish national aspirations in Palestine. Balfour himself was a Christian Zionist who saw Jewish restoration as both spiritually significant and politically beneficial for Britain's interests in the Middle East as the Ottoman Empire collapsed. Remarkably, rather than keeping the prized city holy to Christianity as a jewel in their royal empire, the British Empire was guided by biblically minded individuals like Balfour to immediately return Palestine to the Jews.

After the dust had settled and the winds of war had ceased, the international community gathered in 1920 for the San Remo Conference to formally divide and administer the former territories of the defeated Ottoman Empire. Britain received the Mandate for Palestine, which included the responsibility of implementing the Balfour Declaration, supporting the establishment of a Jewish national home in Palestine. Yet even as Zionism achieved unprecedented international legitimacy, tensions with the local Arab population began to escalate dramatically.

Despite their official promise as outlined in the Balfour Declaration and enshrined at the San Remo Conference, British colonial administrators began undermining their commitments. Eager to maintain access to the recently discovered oil fields throughout the Middle East, British officials became increasingly sympathetic to Arab concerns. Tensions between British promises to the Jews and Arab oil interests would define the next phase of the struggle. The Zionist movement began to prepare for the possibility that their dreams might have to be achieved through force rather than diplomacy.

A devastating turning point was reached in 1929 that shattered illusions about peaceful Jewish and Arab coexistence in Palestine. On August 24, coinciding with Tisha B'Av, the Jewish day of mourning for the destruction of the ancient Temples, Arab riots erupted in Jerusalem following false rumors that Jews were planning to seize control of Muslim holy sites. The violence quickly spread to Hebron, where 67 Jews were brutally murdered in tactics hauntingly similar to both Kishinev in 1903 and the attack from Gaza in 2023.

The Jewish community of Hebron, which had maintained a continuous presence for centuries alongside the Tomb of the Patriarchs where Abraham, Isaac, and Jacob are buried, was effectively destroyed in a single day. Similar attacks in the northern city of Safed claimed 18 Jewish lives, with many others wounded. In acts of barbaric savagery, the violence was particularly shocking as Arab residents turned on their Jewish neighbors, mutilating their victims, burning synagogues and desecrating Torah scrolls.

These attacks left deep psychological scars on the Old Yishuv and demonstrated with horrifying clarity the urgent necessity of developing self-defense capabilities and achieving sovereign statehood. The Jews realized that they could no longer depend on the goodwill of their neighbors or the protection of distant colonial authorities.

Crucially, not all Arabs opposed Jewish settlement in Palestine. In the early years of Zionist immigration, many Arab leaders and communities had welcomed Jewish immigrants, recognizing the economic benefits they brought through investment, modern farming techniques, and job creation. Chaim Weizmann had cultivated positive relationships with moderate Arab leaders who saw potential for cooperation and mutual benefit. The most notable of these relationships was with Emir Faisal, who led the Arab nationalist movement during World War I.

In January 1919, Weizmann and Faisal signed an agreement supporting both Arab independence and Jewish immigration to Palestine, with Faisal writing: "We Arabs look with the deepest sympathy on the Zionist movement... We will wish the Jews a most hearty welcome home." This spirit of cooperation suggested that Arab-Jewish coexistence was not only possible but mutually beneficial.

However, these moderate Arab voices were increasingly drowned out by radical extremists, most notably Haj Amin al-Husseini, who would become one of the most destructive figures in Middle Eastern history. Appointed as Grand Mufti of Jerusalem by the British, Husseini transformed an official religious position into a platform for violent political extremism.

Grand Mufti Haj Amin al-Husseini meeting with Adolf Hitler in November 28, 1941 (Photo by Heinrich Hoffmann)

When elections were held for the role of Grand Mufti in 1921, the unpopular Husseini finished fourth out of four candidates, receiving minimal support from the local Arab population. The three candidates who outpolled him were all moderates who had demonstrated a willingness to work constructively with both the British authorities and the growing Jewish community. However, in a typically short-sighted move, the British overruled the popular vote and appointed Husseini with the naive belief that an extremist nationalist leader would be more effective in controlling the local population than moderate ones. Appointing a radical would backfire spectacularly as Husseini used his British-granted authority not to suppress extremism but to organize and legitimize it on an unprecedented scale.

Husseini was a master of propaganda and incitement who systematically poisoned Arab-Jewish relations through false accusations and religious manipulation. The Islamic cleric used his bully pulpit to spread inflammatory rumors about Jewish plans to destroy the Al-Aqsa Mosque, organized boycotts of Jewish businesses, and established terror groups to attack Old Yishuv settlements.

The Arab Revolt of 1936-1939 represented the culmination of Husseini's radical agenda, as he provoked Arab passions from a general labor strike into a full-scale armed rebellion that targeted both British authorities and Jewish settlements. Husseini orchestrated this uprising, demonstrating how a fanatical extremist could hijack an entire national movement, drowning out moderate voices and making compromise impossible.

Meanwhile, across Europe, the rise of Adolf Hitler in Germany was transforming the continent into an increasingly dangerous place for Jewish life. Hitler's Nazi Party, which had come to power in 1933, was systematically stripping Jews of their civil rights, their property, and ultimately their lives. The Nuremberg Laws of 1935 had legally codified Jewish persecution, and by the late 1930s, the situation deteriorated so much that synagogues were being openly burned, while masses of Jews desperately sought escape from the growing continent-wide catastrophe.

With the specter of another devastating war in Europe looming ever more dangerously, and facing pressure from the threat of further Arab violence in Palestine, Britain made a series of fateful decisions that would fundamentally alter the Middle Eastern landscape. The architect of these policies was Neville Chamberlain, who had become Prime Minister in 1937 and brought to Middle Eastern affairs the same philosophy of appeasement that would soon prove so disastrous in dealing with Hitler. Chamberlain believed that British interests would best be served by avoiding confrontation wherever possible, even if this meant betraying previous commitments and rewarding aggression.

By 1939, the British government added to the abandonment of the Jews by publishing the White Paper. The document doomed the Jews by effectively cancelling the Balfour Declaration and rejecting all hopes for Jewish self-governance in Palestine. The White Paper's provisions were devastating in their scope and timing, drastically limiting Jewish immigration to just 75,000 people over five years. Land sales to Jews were also severely restricted across the country. Most alarmingly, the White Paper envisioned Palestine evolving into an Arab-majority independent state, ensuring that Jews would become a permanent minority in their ancestral homeland, a death knell for Jewish statehood.

Just as he had sought to appease Hitler at Munich in 1938, sacrificing Czechoslovakia in the vain hope of avoiding war, with the White Paper, Chamberlain sought to appease Arab extremists by sacrificing Jewish rights in Palestine. In both cases, Britain betrayed its commitments to democratic allies in the futile hope of buying peace from totalitarian aggressors. Concessions to Hitler had not prevented World War II but had emboldened Nazi aggression, while betraying the Jews in Palestine had not brought peace with the Arabs, but had rewarded extremism and violence. The deadly consequences of appeasement would soon become apparent as the Nazi Holocaust consumed European Jewry while the doors to Palestine remained locked by British policy.

Britian's policy reversal came at a time when European Jews were facing their darkest hour. Nazi persecution was escalating rapidly beyond anyone's worst fears. The infamous Kristallnacht pogrom of November 1938 had seen hundreds of synagogues, Jewish homes and businesses burned throughout Germany and Austria. Jewish children were expelled from schools and Jewish families stripped of their citizenship and property.

By 1939, it was becoming clear that the Nazi regime was preparing something far worse than persecution. Hitler was planning the complete elimination of European Jewry, and the timing could not have been more catastrophically cruel. Just when millions of European Jews were condemned to death with no escape routes available, Britain slammed shut the one remaining door to safety. The Jewish national home that had been promised as a refuge from persecution was now declared off-limits to the very people who needed it most desperately.

Ze'ev Jabotinsky, who had long warned of the need for Jewish self-reliance and military preparedness, captured the agony of this moment in words that proved chillingly prescient. Speaking on Tisha B'Av 1938, as the storm clouds gathered over Europe, Jabotinsky declared with desperate urgency, "It is already the eleventh hour... I see the fire engulfing our people, and I demand that we save what can be saved." He continued with a warning to European Jews, "Liquidate the exile before the exile liquidates you!"

A NEW LEADER FOR DESPERATE TIMES

Extraordinary times require extraordinary leaders, and in the wake of Theodor Herzl's untimely death in 1904, the Jewish people were blessed with a visionary who would prove equal to the monumental challenges ahead. David Ben-Gurion (1886-1973) was born David Gruen in the small town of Płońsk, then part of the Russian Empire. His father, Avigdor, was a Hebrew teacher and early Zionist who instilled in his son both a love of Jewish learning and a commitment to Jewish national revival.

David absorbed his father's passion for Zionism, but unlike the older generation of armchair nationalists, he was determined to build the Jewish state with his own hands. At the age of twenty, inspired by Herzl's movement and driven by an insatiable sense of personal mission, Ben-Gurion made aliyah to Palestine in 1906 with the Second Aliyah. From the moment he set foot on the soil of the ancient homeland, he regarded himself as personally responsible for the fate of the

Jewish people, a burden he would carry for the rest of his life.

Ben-Gurion threw himself into the backbreaking labor of agricultural settlement, working in the orange groves and vineyards of the kibbutzim that were transforming the landscape of Palestine. But even as he toiled in the fields, Ben-Gurion's mind was focused on larger questions of Jewish national development. He quickly became involved in Jewish governance, recognizing that the future state would need experienced leaders who understood both the practical challenges of building a society and the political complexities of achieving independence.

Ben-Gurion understood intuitively what Herzl had grasped intellectually and would remark, "It doesn't matter what the gentiles say; what matters is what the Jews do." Jewish statehood would ultimately depend not on the promises of foreign governments but on the Jews creating facts on the ground that would make independence inevitable.

Despite the critical challenges presented by British betrayal and the deteriorating situation in Europe, Zionists doubled down on the urgent development of institutional infrastructure for their state-in-waiting. They refused to allow British hostility or Arab violence to derail their preparations for the independence they knew would eventually come.

The World Zionist Organization's Jewish Agency, which was recognized by the international community as the official representative body of Jewish interests in Palestine, functioned effectively as a provisional government under Ben-Gurion's increasingly dominant leadership. The changing relationship between the World Zionist Organization (WZO) and the Jewish Agency (JA) reflected the evolution of Zionist institutions since Herzl's death.

The WZO, established at the First Zionist Congress in 1897, remained the global umbrella body coordinating Zionist activities worldwide and coordinated fundraising, advocacy, and political activities across the globe. However, as the practical work of building a Jewish society in Palestine intensified, the need arose for a more focused executive body. The JA was created in 1929 and specifically tasked with implementing Zionist policy in Palestine itself, concentrating on the day-to-day work of immigration absorption, land settlement, and institution building. This was no longer the amateur enthusiasm of idealistic intellectuals, but the professional competence of a government-in-exile preparing to assume full sovereignty.

Ben-Gurion's rise to leadership of the Jewish Agency came through his combination of practical experience, political acumen, and unmatched dedication to the Zionist cause. Unlike Weizmann, who spent most of his time in London and Paris, Ben-Gurion lived in Palestine, spoke Hebrew fluently, and understood intimately the challenges facing Jewish settlers. His election as chairman of the Jewish Agency Executive in 1935 marked his emergence as the de facto leader of Palestinian Jewry and the architect of Jewish independence.

An autodidact who read voraciously in multiple languages, Ben-Gurion mastered ancient Greek to read Plato and Aristotle in the original. In addition to his intellectual gifts, he developed into one of the most articulate and compelling orators on behalf of Political Zionism. His speeches combined philosophical depth with practical urgency, biblical imagery with contemporary political analysis. He could quote from the Hebrew prophets and Greek philosophers with equal facility, then pivot seamlessly to discussing immigration quotas and land purchases.

As reports of Nazi atrocities began filtering through to Palestine, Ben-Gurion's rhetoric took on an increasingly desperate edge. In a searing speech delivered in 1942, he lashed out at British policy with particular fury:

"We do not know exactly what goes on in the Nazi valley of death, or how many Jews have already been slaughtered. As long as the gates to our land are closed, your hands, too, [Britain] will be steeped in Jewish blood. What has happened to us in Poland, what God forbid, will happen to us in the future, all our innocent victims, all the tens of thousands, hundreds of thousands, and perhaps millions, are the sacrifices of a people without a homeland. We demand a homeland and independence!"

When news of the Holocaust's unprecedented scale became undeniable, Zionist leaders faced an impossible moral dilemma. Should they focus all their energies on winning the war against Hitler, or should they divert resources to fight British immigration restrictions that were condemning countless Jews to death? The tension was agonizing, but Ben-Gurion resolved it with characteristic clarity and determination.

Like their predecessors in World War I, the Jews aligned themselves decisively with the Allies against Nazi Germany. Tens of thousands of Jews enlisted in British and American armies, fighting on multiple fronts from North Africa to Europe. Simultaneously, the Zionists organized daring rescue operations and resistance efforts that demonstrated their refusal to remain passive victims of either Nazi genocide or British indifference.

One of the most inspiring examples of Jewish heroism during this period was Hannah Szenes, a young Hungarian Jew who had escaped to Palestine in 1939 and joined Kibbutz Sdot Yam. Despite her safety in Palestine, Szenes volunteered for a dangerous mission to parachute behind enemy lines in Nazi-occupied Europe to help organize Jewish resistance and rescue operations. Captured by the Nazis, Szenes was tortured and executed at the age of twenty-three, but not before becoming a symbol of Jewish courage and the lengths to which Palestinian Jews would go to save their brethren in Europe. Her haunting poem captures the spirit of Jewish resistance during those dark years: "Blessed is the match consumed by a kindling flame."

With very limited resources and facing overwhelming British opposition, Zionists mounted increasingly daring rescue operations and organized clandestine immigration networks to break the blockade of Palestine. Between 1939 and 1948, approximately 115,000 Jews were smuggled into Palestine despite British naval patrols, internment camps, and deportation policies that sent refugees back to certain death in Europe.

The most infamous incident occurred in 1947 when the ship 'Exodus', carrying 4,500 Holocaust survivors, was violently seized by British forces off the coast of Palestine and its passengers forcibly returned to displaced persons camps in Germany. The former Chesapeake Bay ferry had been purchased by the Haganah and secretly converted to carry refugees. Despite its overcrowded conditions, passengers were packed so tightly they could barely lie down, the ship became a symbol of hope for Holocaust survivors desperate to reach Palestine.

When British destroyers surrounded the vessel eighteen miles off the Palestinian coast, passengers and crew fought back with anything they could get their hands on including canned food, potatoes, and improvised weapons. British sailors boarded the 'Exodus' with clubs and tear gas, killing three passengers and wounding dozens more in full view of international journalists who had been invited aboard to witness the confrontation. The sight of Jewish Holocaust survivors being beaten by British forces, then shipped back to internment camps in Germany, created a public relations catastrophe for Britain and transformed international opinion decisively in favor of Jewish independence.

Ben-Gurion captured the moral complexity of Jewish resistance to the British during this period with a formula that became legendary, "We shall fight the war as if there were no White Paper, and the White Paper as if there were no war." This seemingly contradictory approach reflected the Zionist movement's refusal to choose between fighting Hitler and fighting for Jewish survival. They would do both simultaneously, regardless of the cost.

The explosion of antisemitism that Herzl had witnessed during the Dreyfus Affair reached its horrific climax in World War II. What had begun as social prejudice and political discrimination evolved into systematic genocide as Adolf Hitler's Nazi regime attempted to solve the "Jewish Question" through mass murder. The Holocaust was not merely a German initiative but a European one, carried out with the willing assistance of collaborators across the continent. From the streets of Paris to the villages of Poland, from the universities of Holland to the courtyards of Hungary, millions of European Christians participated in or remained silent about the systematic destruction of their Jewish neighbors.

The churches, which might have provided moral leadership, largely failed their fundamental test. Pope Pius XII maintained his silence even as cattle cars carrying crying Jewish children passed beneath the Vatican windows. While there were individual Righteous Gentiles, Christians who risked their lives to save Jews, they were heroic exceptions that highlighted the moral failure of the majority. Despite their courage and sacrifice, which saved thousands of Jewish lives, it was not enough. Six million Jews were murdered, including 1.5 million children, in the most systematic genocide in human history.

The Holocaust represents both the nadir of Jewish history and the tragic validation of Zionist arguments about the necessity of Jewish statehood. The brutal murder of one-third of the world's Jewish population, demonstrated with horrific finality the vulnerability of Jewish existence in the Diaspora. No amount of assimilation, no level of patriotism, no degree of cultural contribution could provide lasting security for Jews living as minorities in gentile societies.

The *Shoah* (Holocaust) transformed Zionism from but one of several possible solutions to the "Jewish Question" into an urgent moral imperative that could no longer be ignored or postponed. The devastating loss of European Jewry created a sense of urgency that galvanized both Jewish determination and international sympathy. Many who had previously been indifferent or opposed to Jewish nationalism now recognized the absolute necessity of a Jewish state as insurance against future genocides.

The immediate post-World War II period saw the Zionist movement simultaneously pursuing three interconnected campaigns: continued illegal immigration of Holocaust survivors desperate to reach Palestine, intensified diplomatic efforts to secure international recognition of Jewish statehood, and escalating military resistance to British rule that would force the issue to a definitive conclusion.

The stage was set for the final confrontation that would determine whether Herzl's vision would finally become reality or whether it would die with the six million who had been denied refuge in their ancestral homeland.

Cruelly, after World War II ended, Britain strengthened restrictions on Jewish immigration, continuing to prevent Holocaust survivors from entering Palestine even as the full horror of Nazi genocide became clear. As desperate survivors languished in displaced persons camps across Europe, the moral bankruptcy of British immigration restrictions became increasingly apparent, barring the doors on what was meant to be a refuge for persecuted Jews.

In a revealing speech to the British Parliament in February 1947, Foreign Secretary Ernest Bevin inadvertently clarified the fundamental nature of the conflict when he explained Britain's inability to maintain its authority in Palestine. Bevin acknowledged that the conflict was not a dispute between two comparable national movements seeking their respective independence. "For the Jews," Bevin observed, "the essential point of principle is the creation of a sovereign Jewish State. For the Arabs, the essential point of principle is to resist to the last the establishment of Jewish sovereignty in any part of Palestine."

This stark assessment revealed the asymmetry that would define the conflict for generations. While Palestine's Jews sought to build, Palestine's Arabs sought only to destroy. As Jews were willing to make diplomatic compromises on territory and borders, Arabs rejected any Jewish presence whatsoever. Britain, exhausted by war and facing mounting costs and casualties in the Middle East, announced it would terminate its mandate and transfer the Palestine question to the newly formed United Nations.

The UN appointed a Special Committee on Palestine (UNSCOP) to investigate the situation and recommend a solution. After extensive deliberation, the committee recommended partitioning the territory into separate Jewish and Arab states, with Jerusalem placed under international administration. On November 29, 1947, the UN General Assembly voted 33 to 13, with 10 abstentions, to adopt and implement the partition plan.

Map of UN Partition Plan for Palestine adopted in November 1947

Despite the fact that the proposed Jewish state had been dramatically reduced in size, comprising only a narrow strip of coastal plain and the Negev desert, the desperate Jews accepted UNSCOP's partition plan. The Arabs, however, categorically rejected the notion of any Jewish state, regardless of how small, and immediately launched an all-out assault against Jewish communities throughout Palestine. From the very beginning, the Arab position was clear: their goal was never to establish an Arab state alongside a Jewish one, but to block a Jewish state.

"TO BE CALLED THE STATE OF ISRAEL"

As British soldiers lowered the Union Jack for the final time and the British Mandate officially expired, David Ben-Gurion stood before a crowded gathering in the Tel Aviv Museum on Friday afternoon, May 14, 1948, and proclaimed independence. At that very moment, Jerusalem was cut off and under siege by Arab forces with no electricity, symbolizing the precarious circumstances surrounding the birth of the Jewish state.

In his historic speech, Ben-Gurion declared:

> "*Eretz Israel* (the Land of Israel) was the birthplace of the Jewish people. Here their spiritual, religious and political identity was shaped. Here they first attained statehood, created cultural values of national and universal significance and gave to the world the eternal Book of Books.

> After being forcibly exiled from their land, the people kept faith with it throughout their Dispersion and never ceased to pray and hope for their return to it and for the restoration in it of their political freedom . . .

> This right is the natural right of the Jewish people to be masters of their own fate, like all other nations, in their own sovereign State.

> Accordingly we, members of the People's Council, representatives of the Jewish community of *Eretz Israel* and of the Zionist movement, are here assembled on the day of the termination of the British Mandate over *Eretz Israel* and, by virtue of our natural and historic right and on the strength of the resolution of the United Nations General Assembly, hereby declare the establishment of a Jewish State in *Eretz Israel*, to be known as the State of Israel."

Following the proclamation, the assembled delegates rose for the recitation of the traditional *Shehechiyanu* blessing, "Blessed are You, Lord our God, King of the universe, who has granted us life, sustained us, and enabled us to reach this occasion, Amen."

Controversially, despite this moment of profound historical significance for the Jewish people to finally become "like all other nations", Israel's Declaration of Independence contained no mention of God, a reflection of the Political Zionist leadership's ambivalence about the religious dimensions of Jewish restoration.

David Ben-Gurion declaring the independence of the State of Israel (Photo by Rudi Weissenstein, May 1948)

Within minutes of Ben-Gurion's proclamation, President Harry Truman became the first world leader to recognize the new state, acting against the counsel of his State Department advisors who warned of dire consequences for American interests in the Arab world. Truman, a lifelong Bible student who kept a map of ancient Palestine on his White House wall, believed he had been placed in his position for this historic moment.

When Chief Rabbi Isaac Halevi Herzog visited the White House to thank the President for recognizing Israel, he presented Truman with a Torah scroll as a gift. Rabbi Herzog told the President, "God put you in your mother's womb so you would be the instrument to bring about Israel's rebirth." Upon hearing these words, Truman wept. On another occasion, when a supporter compared him to the Persian King Cyrus mentioned in the Bible for allowing the Jewish exiles to return to Jerusalem and rebuild their Temple, Truman responded with enthusiasm, "I am Cyrus! I am Cyrus!" For Truman, who didn't go to college but grew up reading the Bible, recognizing Israel was not merely a political calculation but the fulfillment of what he believed to be his God-given destiny.

Upon announcing its independence, spontaneous celebrations erupted in the streets of Tel Aviv and Jewish communities around the world, yet Ben-Gurion remained grimly realistic about the challenges ahead. That night, he wrote in his diary: "Everybody was happy, and I... was heavy-hearted. I knew that we would be at war the next day."

Ben-Gurion's prediction proved tragically accurate. Within hours of Israel's Declaration of Independence, the well-equipped armies of five Arab countries - Egypt, Syria, Transjordan, Lebanon, and Iraq - invaded the newborn state with the explicit goal of destroying it before it could take root. Arab League Secretary-General Azzam Pasha declared with malice, "This will be a war of extermination and momentous massacre which will be spoken of like the Mongolian massacre and the Crusades."

The War of Independence raged for fifteen months. Despite devastating initial setbacks and being drastically outnumbered and outgunned, Israeli forces gradually gained the upper hand through superior organization, motivation, and the desperate knowledge that defeat meant annihilation. By early 1949, armistice agreements had been signed with each Arab state, though significantly, the Arabs refused to sign actual peace treaties with the Jewish State.

The war's outcome was mixed for Israel. The new state successfully defended a core territory, but tragically lost control of Judaism's holiest sites. The Old City of Jerusalem, with the Western Wall and Temple Mount, fell to Jordanian forces, as did the biblically significant regions of Judea and Samaria. Since Judea and Samaria lay outside the original territory of Transjordan, when King Abdullah announced their annexation in 1950, only two countries in the entire world recognized this illegal occupation, Britain and Pakistan. By and large, the international community understood that Jordan had no legitimate claim to the biblical heartland of the Jewish people, territories that had been designated for Jewish settlement by international consensus.

With independence achieved against impossible odds, Zionism faced an immediate and dramatic transition from state-creation to state-building. Three enormous challenges confronted the infant nation: absorbing massive immigration, establishing functioning governance, and maintaining security against implacably hostile neighbors.

Immediately after adopting the Declaration of Independence, the new Israeli government unanimously abolished the despised White Paper of 1939 and threw open the borders of the Jewish state to unlimited Jewish immigration. Between May 1948 and December 1951, Israel's Jewish population doubled from approximately 650,000 to 1.3 million people. This extraordinary demographic transformation included both survivors of the Holocaust from Europe, many bearing physical and psychological scars from their ordeal, and Jewish refugees from Arab countries who arrived with little more than the clothes on their backs after being violently expelled from homes their families had occupied for generations.

To accommodate this unprecedented influx, the Israeli government established temporary transit camps, called *ma'abarot*, while racing to construct permanent housing. The financial burden was crushing, necessitating severe austerity measures, food rationing, and substantial foreign assistance, particularly from American Jewish organizations that mobilized resources on an unprecedented scale.

David Ben-Gurion, who had served as the head of the Jewish Agency, attempted to close down the World Zionist Organization and its pre-state institutions, folding them into the new government. He understood that it would be a mistake to allow a shadow government to continue alongside the new state agencies. However, strong pushback from the anti-Zionist elements that remained from the days of Herzl, and from wealthy American Jewish donors, led Ben-Gurion to back down from his demands. As a result, massive land holdings would remain in the hands of Keren Kayemet L'Yisrael (the Jewish National Fund) and not become state property. The first Prime Minister had many other raging fires to put out, and as a result, the World Zionist Organization evolved to support the new reality.

The Jewish Agency's role shifted from underground coordination to promoting legal immigration and absorption services. Jewish fundraising organizations channeled diaspora support toward development projects, while American Jews and Christians organized to lobby for favorable policies toward the embryonic State of Israel.

LIMITATIONS OF POLITICAL ZIONISM

The transformation of Zionism from visionary movement to sovereign state power, achieved against overwhelming odds between 1897 and 1948, represents one of the most extraordinary political accomplishments in human history. Yet this remarkable success came with significant limitations that would become increasingly apparent in subsequent decades.

Critics of Political Zionism, both within Israel and abroad, point to several fundamental shortcomings that political independence alone could not address.

Economic Struggles: Despite achieving statehood, Israel faced severe poverty and economic hardship that persisted for decades. The burden of absorbing massive immigration while simultaneously building a modern economy from scratch proved nearly overwhelming.

Internal Division: From the very beginning, deep ideological rifts divided the Zionist movement. Reform and Orthodoxy overwhelmingly rejected Zionism, while Cultural Zionists like Ahad Ha'am warned that political achievements without cultural renewal would prove hollow. Religious Zionists argued that secular nationalism could never satisfy the deeper longings of the Jewish soul.

Rising Anti-Zionism: Perhaps most troubling, Herzl's confident prediction that Jewish statehood would eliminate antisemitism proved tragically false. Instead of ending Jew-hatred, Israel's establishment seemed only to provide it with a new focus.

Yet for all its limitations, the reestablishment of Jewish sovereignty provides humanity with a unique test case. As Benjamin Netanyahu observed in his book *A Place Among the Nations*:

> "Now the Jews have entered a new phase in their history. Since the rise of Israel, the essence of their aspirations has changed. If the central aim of the Jewish people during its exile was to retrieve what had been lost, the purpose now is to secure what has been retrieved. It is a task that has barely begun, and its outcome is of profound import, not only for the fate of the Jews, but for all mankind."

Benjamin Netanyahu, who began this chapter by identifying King Saul as his biblical hero and Theodor Herzl as his political inspiration, understood that securing Israel's place required something more profound than military strength or economic success. He concluded with words that pointed toward a greater destiny:

> "If, echoing the words of the prophet Amos, the fallen tent of David has indeed risen again, its resurrection is proof that there is hope for every people in every nation under the sun... It is the incomparable quest of a people seeking, at the end of an unending march, to assume its rightful place among the nations."

The progression from King Saul to Herzl to Ben-Gurion to Netanyahu represents the brilliant fulfillment of Political Zionism's essential mission.

The ancient Israelites' request to Samuel, to "give us a king to govern us like all the other nations," found its modern echo in Herzl's desire for Jews to achieve "normalization" among the family of nations. Herzl had created the institutional framework of a government-in-exile, complete with congresses, flags, and anthems, all the trappings of a legitimate state. Ben-Gurion fought ferociously for "the Jewish people to be masters of their own fate, like all other nations" and Netanyahu has presided over Israel's emergence as a regional power that has finally achieved its "rightful place among the nations."

Just as King Saul's political achievements had laid the groundwork for King David's spiritual renaissance, Political Zionism's success would make possible the next stage in the drama of Jewish restoration, one that would build upon Political Zionism's temporal achievements while transcending its material limitations.

Yet the very success of Political Zionism revealed its inherent limitations. Israel had built a body, but it still needed a soul.

The country could defend itself against larger countries militarily and compete with older nations economically, but it struggled to articulate a compelling vision of why its existence mattered beyond Jewish survival. The goal of being "like all other nations" has been largely achieved, but this raises a deeper question: Is survival the ultimate purpose of Jewish restoration?

The next phase of Israel's development would discover that the true goal was not to be like all others, but to be a nation *unlike* all other nations.

RELIGIOUS ZIONISM

3

RELIGIOUS ZIONISM

As Netanyahu observed, King Saul was indeed a tragic figure. Despite his remarkable achievements in uniting the twelve tribes and establishing Israel's first monarchy, Saul's reign ended tragically because he repeatedly placed his own judgment above divine instruction.

When ordered to completely destroy the evil Amalekites, he showed what seemed like merciful restraint by sparing their King Agag and the best of their livestock. Saul's misplaced compassion would have catastrophic consequences, as he himself died by the sword of an Amalekite (II Samuel 1), while Israel's nemesis continued to harass future generations of the Jewish people (Esther 3:1). King Saul's lack of perfect faith led him to substitute his own morality for God's explicit commandments, demonstrating the fundamental flaw that would ultimately cost him his kingdom.

In the ruthless world of politics, success is measured by one's ability to acquire and maintain power, and throughout his reign, King Saul became increasingly desperate in his efforts to cling to his throne. Rather than taking pride in his tremendous accomplishments from uniting the fractious tribes into a coherent kingdom, building the initial political infrastructure, and successfully defending Israel against existential threats, Saul became consumed with jealousy and paranoia as a potential successor emerged.

When David appeared as the divinely chosen leader of the next generation, rather than gracefully recognizing David's unique gifts, Saul sank into depressive episodes. The first king spent his final years obsessively hunting David across the wilderness, trying to eliminate the very person God had chosen to be the second king and complete what Saul had begun.

David's response to Saul's murderous pursuits revealed not weakness but a potential for greatness. Where an ordinary man might have rallied his supporters for an insurrection, David responded with magnanimity preserving his own integrity and the dignity of the still-fragile monarchy. He recognized that Israel's kingship was too new and too precious to be damaged by internal strife, and so rather than confronting Saul directly, he chose exile. Instead of trying to turn Saul's family against him, David cultivated deep friendships with Jonathan and married Michal, maintaining ties to Saul's son and daughter that would serve to strengthen rather than divide the kingdom.

Like Saul before him, David was a devoted shepherd from a modest family, hardly the most obvious candidate for kingship. David did, at least, come from the tribe of Judah, which had received Jacob's blessing centuries earlier, "The scepter shall not depart from Judah" (Genesis 49:10). Still, David was the youngest son in a large family, so insignificant that when Samuel arrived to anoint one of Jesse's offspring as the next king, his own father didn't even bother to call him in from the fields. "Are these all the young men?" Samuel asked, and Jesse replied, "There remains yet the youngest, but behold, he is tending the sheep" (1 Samuel 16:11). Yet Samuel, who had earlier recognized something special in Saul despite his humble origins, now discerned the hand of God pointing toward this unlikely shepherd boy. When David finally appeared ruddy-faced, bright-eyed, and handsome, the Lord told Samuel, "Arise, anoint him, for this is he" (1 Samuel 16:12).

DAVID MY SERVANT

Like Saul before him, David kept his anointing a secret, waiting for God's timing to reveal his destiny. That moment came when the Philistines once again threatened Israel, this time through their champion Goliath, a giant of a man whose bronze armor and iron spear made him seemingly invincible.

For forty days, Goliath taunted the Israelite army, challenging them to send a fighter to face him in single combat. While seasoned warriors cowered in their tents, young David, who had come to the battlefield merely to bring food for his older brothers, volunteered to face the giant that had paralyzed Israel's entire army.

Like Saul before him, David proved his qualifications on the battlefield, but here is where the similarities between the two kings end. When confronted by the enemy, Saul viewed the Philistines' provocations as an attempt to "defy Israel," referring primarily to the nation and its people (1 Samuel 17:25). David, however, perceived these insults as an affront to God Himself. "Who is this uncircumcised Philistine," he demanded, "that he dares to defy the ranks of the living God?" (1 Samuel 17:26).

From David's perspective, the nation of Israel was, above all, a manifestation of Divine Providence, and the life of the nation was inextricably linked to and sustained by God. Accordingly, during his reign, the spiritual renewal of the nation would take precedence over material development, a revolutionary approach that would later define the unique role Religious Zionism would play at a later stage in history.

Upon confronting the giant, David immediately and instinctively gave credit for his victory to the Almighty. Standing before Goliath, David declared with absolute confidence, "You come to me with sword and spear and javelin, but I come to you in the name of the Lord of hosts, the God of the armies of Israel," (1 Samuel 17:45). David transformed a moment of national military crisis into an opportunity for religious inspiration, turning the hearts of his people toward the God of Israel.

Unlike Saul, this spiritual dimension and instinctive recognition that every challenge was ultimately about Israel's relationship with God, separated David not only from Saul before him, but from every subsequent king in Israel's history. As a result, David was in a cherished league of his own.

In Hebrew, the root word D-V-D means beloved, and David was favored by the Lord. He is "a man after God's own heart" (1 Samuel 13:14) and "successful in all his ways, and God was with him" (1 Samuel 18:14). The feeling was mutual.

David was, first and foremost, a man who was always thinking about God, talking to God, singing to God, and praising God, "I have set the Lord always before me" (Psalms 16:8). His psalms would become the prayer book of humanity, expressing the full range of human emotion in relationship with the divine for all time. The contrast between the two kings became even more apparent in their attitudes toward Israel's most sacred symbol.

Unlike Saul, David was deeply troubled by the fate of the Ark of the Covenant, which had been captured by the Philistines years earlier. While Saul had shown no particular concern for the Ark's absence and made no effort to restore it to its proper place in Israel's religious life, David made its recovery a national priority.

When he finally succeeded in bringing the Ark back to Jerusalem, "David danced with all of his strength before God" (2 Samuel 6:14), celebrating with uninhibited joy. King David's unbridled display scandalized his wife Michal, Saul's daughter, who was unable to appreciate such religious ecstasy, but revealed the depth of David's spiritual devotion.

David's choice of Jerusalem as his capital demonstrated the same spiritual intuition that characterized all his major decisions. Rather than selecting a city from his own tribal territory of Judah, he chose the Jebusite stronghold perched on the hills between Judah and Benjamin. The neutral location, "Jerusalem, built as a city that is united together" (Psalm 122:3) would symbolize unity between his own administration and that of his predecessor. But David's vision for Jerusalem extended beyond political symbolism to religious significance.

David was deeply troubled that his new capital lacked a proper dwelling place for God:

> "It happened after the king was settled into his home and God had given him respite from his enemies all around, that the king said to Nathan the prophet, 'See now, I am dwelling in a house of cedar while the Ark of God dwells within the curtain!'" (2 Samuel 7:1-2)

This inequality weighed heavily on David's conscience, for he was always concerned with God's glory above his own. He desperately wanted to build a monumental Temple worthy of his beloved Creator, a structure that would serve as the focal point for Israel's spiritual life.

Yet when David shared his vision with the prophet Nathan, God's response revealed a divine plan for Israel's slow and gradual development. "When your days are done, and you lie with your fathers, I will raise up your offspring after you, one of your own issue, and I will establish his kingship. He shall build a house for My name, and I will establish his throne forever" (2 Samuel 7:12-13).

During King David's reign, the *Beit Hamikdash* (Temple) was conceived as a national vision, but it would not be built because David and the nation were not yet ready for such a momentous undertaking.

David's legacy lay not in the Temple he didn't build, but in the spiritual foundation he established. Namely, the recognition that Israel's ultimate purpose transcended political survival and material prosperity. He had taken the physical body of Saul's material achievement and breathed into it a soul, transforming Israel from merely another kingdom among the nations into a people whose very existence testified to the reality of God's presence in human history.

This pattern of the physical preceding the spiritual echoes throughout Tanakh, most vividly in Ezekiel's vision of the valley of dry bones. In that symbolic vision representing the ultimate resurrection of Israel, the prophet witnessed scattered and brittle dry bones, "and behold a commotion, and the bones came together bone to bone." Only when the bodies were formed, did God tell Ezekiel to bring about the next step, "So I prophesied as He commanded me, and the breath came into them, and they lived, and stood up upon their feet, an exceedingly great host" (Ezekiel 37:7,10).

The same paradigm would repeat itself in modern times, as Religious Zionism would build upon the political foundations laid by Herzl and Ben-Gurion, discovering that Jewish statehood was not an end in itself but the essential prerequisite for spiritual renewal. Like the progression from Political to Religious to

Universal Zionism in modern times, the ancient Israelite kingdom required careful preparation through successive phases. It would take the next generation of Solomon to fulfill the sacred stage that could transform both Israel and the world.

PREVENTING THE MESSIAH

While the establishment of the State of Israel after half a century of seemingly miraculous developments from Herzl to Ben-Gurion might have been expected to resonate with all Torah-faithful Jews, this was emphatically not the case. Many ultra-Orthodox and Hasidic Jews not only failed to appreciate Zionism, they saw it as spiritually dangerous. No one represents Torah-based opposition to Zionism more than Rabbi Yoel Teitelbaum, known as the Satmar Rebbe.

In the dark days of 1944, as the gas chambers and crematoria of Auschwitz were operating at their deadliest capacity, consuming up to ten thousand Jewish lives each day, the tide was turning against Nazi Germany. Desperate for funds and resources, the Nazis became willing to negotiate deals that might have seemed unthinkable earlier in their campaign of extermination. At great personal risk, Rudolf Kasztner, a Zionist activist, negotiated one of the war's most controversial rescue operations by bribing Nazi leader Adolf Eichmann to allow 1,600 Hungarian Jews safe passage to Switzerland, sparing them from deportation to Auschwitz. The ransom was enormous: money, gold, and valuables collected from wealthy Jews and Jewish organizations around the world.

Rabbi Yoel Teitelbaum (1887-1979), the revered leader of the Satmar Hasidic dynasty and one of Hungary's most influential religious figures, was given a seat on the "Kasztner train" because of his stature as a prominent community leader. This transport would save his life from the ovens of Auschwitz, allowing him to escape the fate that befell hundreds of thousands of his fellow Hungarian Jews. Yet, when asked about his miraculous rescue in later years, Rabbi Teitelbaum would wave off any mention of Zionist involvement with visible scorn. His survival, he declared emphatically, was not thanks to Ben-Gurion's operatives or Kasztner's negotiations with the devil himself, but to Heaven alone. "It was the hand of God that saved me, not the Zionists."

After the war, rather than moving to the newly established Jewish state, where many Holocaust survivors were building new lives, Rabbi Teitelbaum chose to rebuild his devastated Hasidic community in the Williamsburg section of Brooklyn, New York. From this American exile, he argued with passionate conviction that Zionist statehood had brought unprecedented calamity upon the Jewish people.

Far from seeing Zionist rescue efforts as noble acts of Jewish solidarity, Teitelbaum sometimes described them as the work of "Satan himself," cunningly designed to lure Jews into accepting a false redemption. In fiery sermons delivered from his Brooklyn synagogue and in his theological writings, he argued that, "the founding of the State of Israel by secular and religious Jews, rather than the Messiah, violated fundamental Jewish commandments... the very existence of the State of Israel was actually preventing the Messiah from coming."

This extraordinary position revealed the depths of theological opposition that Zionism faced from significant segments of the traditional Jewish world, opposition that would persist and even intensify as Israel's success became undeniable. This perspective, rooted in Torah interpretation and mystical Jewish sources, was far from unique. It represented the majority view among Hasidic Jews and traced its origins all the way back to Zionism's earliest days, revealing a profound theological fault line that would divide the Jewish world for generations.

As we have seen, Herzl had initially reached out to German rabbis for support, believing that religious leaders would naturally embrace a movement promising to restore the Jews to their biblical homeland. Western European rabbis, products of the Enlightenment who had grown comfortable with their newfound freedoms in modern European society, were more open to modernity than their Eastern European counterparts. Yet even these progressive religious leaders rebuffed Herzl for being too nationalistic, with both Reform and Orthodox rabbis in Western Europe viewing Zionism as a dangerous step backward from the integration they had worked so hard to achieve.

In Eastern Europe, where the Enlightenment had not fully penetrated Jewish society and traditional religious life remained largely intact, the rejection of Zionism was even more vehement, though for entirely different reasons. These insular communities had rejected modernity with fierce determination, embracing Hasidism and other forms of ultra-Orthodoxy as bulwarks against secular assimilation. They saw Herzl's movement not as insufficiently modern, but as dangerously secular.

The Chabad Hasidic movement also rejected Zionism from its very inception. The fifth Lubavitcher Rebbe, Rabbi Sholom Dov Ber Schneerson, who led the movement from 1882 to 1920, warned that Zionists "are far more cunning in their evil" than secular assimilationists precisely because Jewish nationalism could be used to replace Torah study and religious observance as the guiding force in Jewish life.

Where secular assimilation was obviously anti-religious, Zionism presented itself as a form of Jewish revival, making it far more seductive and dangerous to traditional Jewish youth. The Rebbe was not wrong. Countless young Jews, inspired by Zionist idealism, began learning modern Hebrew, embracing secular Jewish nationalism, and moving to the Yishuv, where many abandoned their religious practices entirely. The very success of Zionism in capturing Jewish imagination seemed to validate ultra-Orthodox fears about its spiritual dangers.

These ultra-Orthodox leaders saw something even more sinister in Zionism than secularism. Since the beginning of the exile nearly two millennia earlier, traditional Jews had believed that the Torah's descriptions of a return to Israel would occur only in the messianic era, brought about through God's direct divine intervention. The promises of restoration were understood to refer to some distant future time when the miraculous arrival of the *Mashiach* (Messiah) would gather the scattered Jewish people and carry them "on the wings of eagles" back to Jerusalem. Until that time, Jews were expected to remain passive, praying and waiting for God to fight their battles and orchestrate their redemption.

When Zionism emerged under the leadership of secular figures like Theodor Herzl, a man who kept a Christmas tree and whose own son converted to Christianity, Hasidic rabbis felt certain this could not be the Torah's anticipated redemption. They found abundant sources in the Torah to justify their rejectionism. The Hebrew prophets long accused rebellious Jews of not treating Israel with sufficient holiness, "You defiled My land," accused Jeremiah (2:7), and warned against sinful behavior in "a land that consumes its inhabitants" (Numbers 13:32). No human effort could or should bring about the redemption, only God could accomplish such a miraculous restoration.

As Zionism became increasingly successful, the rhetoric became more heated and the opposition more resolute. "It is because of the Zionists that six million Jews were killed," declared the Satmar Rebbe in one of his controversial pronouncements. According to this line of reasoning, the Zionist movement had provoked divine wrath by attempting to force the end of exile prematurely, and the Holocaust was God's punishment for this transgression. By trying to solve the Jewish problem through human political action rather than waiting for divine redemption, the Zionists had brought catastrophe upon the entire Jewish people.

These extreme forms of religious anti-Zionism saw the movement as a profound spiritual danger on multiple levels. Not only did Zionism threaten to pull their children away from traditional faith by offering an attractive secular alternative, it also presented an entirely new model for messianic fulfillment that contradicted their fundamental understanding of how redemption would unfold. For ultra-Orthodox Jews, Judaism was fulfilled through the intensive study and meticulous observance of Torah law as expressed in the Talmud: "From the time of the destruction of the Temple, the only way to approach God is through the practice of *Halacha* (Jewish law)."

According to this worldview, attempting to settle the land prematurely could upset the delicate spiritual dynamic that God had established following the destruction of the Second Temple. Jewish prayers stated, "Because of our sins we were exiled from our land," and until they repented properly and achieved complete atonement for those transgressions, they would remain in exile.

Additionally, Jewish sources spoke of a divine pact with the gentile nations, sealed by three sacred oaths: (1) the nations would not persecute the Jews excessively, (2) the Jews would obey the gentiles, and (3) would not "go up like a wall" to reclaim their land or attempt to bring about the end of days prematurely. Any violation of these oaths would result in catastrophic consequences, they warned.

Therefore, many ultra-Orthodox leaders concluded, the secular Zionist movement was not the fulfillment of biblical prophecy but rather the handiwork of dark spiritual forces that must be resisted at all costs. The very success of Zionism only proved its dangerous nature, as it seduced Jews away from their true calling of religious devotion. These views continue to be held by a significant portion of ultra-Orthodox and Hasidic Jews today, who number in the millions worldwide and represent the fastest-growing sects within the global Jewish population.

However, while the vast majority of traditional rabbis opposed Zionism for numerous and varied theological reasons, there was one remarkable rabbi who saw things very differently. Rabbi Abraham Isaac Kook would revolutionize religious thinking about Jewish restoration and, by developing the philosophy of Religious Zionism, lay the foundation for an entirely new understanding of how God works through history to fulfill His ancient promises.

THE NEW WILL BECOME HOLY

An outstanding Torah scholar and mystic, Rabbi Abraham Isaac Kook (known primarily as Rav Kook) joined the wave of Jewish immigrants to Palestine at the outset of the Second Aliyah in 1904. Impressed by the Jewish revolution beginning to take shape with young pioneers draining malarial swamps, building new towns, and speaking Hebrew for the first time in two millennia, Rav Kook saw something his rabbinical colleagues had missed.

With exceptional literary gifts and mystical insight, Kook produced profound writings in direct opposition to those who denied any spiritual significance to Jewish resettlement in the Holy Land. Where others saw religious dangers, he perceived God's hand behind the scenes and commented about the secular pioneers, "That which is holy will become renewed and that which is new will become holy." While an outlier, Kook wasn't the first rabbinic thinker to see spiritual meaning in the return to the Land of Israel. Two visionary rabbis had laid crucial groundwork decades earlier.

Writing from his small community in Serbia, Rabbi Yehuda Alkalai (1798-1878), mentioned earlier, was the first to envision a natural path towards salvation, rather than a supernatural one. Already in 1843 he declared that, "The Holy One, Blessed be He, will accomplish the redemption by means of diplomacy and respect, through application of the political art." Alkalai went further and condemned those who "maintain that the Messiah will arrive on celestial clouds" as guilty of "a grave sin."

For centuries, Jews had believed just that. Namely, that their return to the Holy Land would come only through miraculous divine intervention, and that the Messiah would actually come down on literal clouds of glory to gather the scattered exiles. Alkalai was arguing the exact opposite by saying that human initiative was not just permitted but required. Jews must be active participants in their own redemption, not passive recipients waiting for God's rescue.

Picking up this revolutionary theme was Rabbi Zvi Hirsch Kalischer (1795–1874), an Orthodox rabbi from Prussia. Unlike many rabbis who lived entirely within the world of Torah study, Kalischer absorbed Enlightenment ideas and was simultaneously troubled by the persecution afflicting European Jews. In his landmark book *Drishat Zion* (Seeking Zion) published in 1862, he urged Jews to return to the Land of Israel, buy property, and establish agricultural colonies. Kalischer taught that settlement of the Land was a religious duty that would hasten the coming of the Messiah.

While most rabbis of his time opposed any practical attempts at redemption, Kalischer believed Jews must work through natural means, supported by Jewish philanthropy. He directly appealed to wealthy figures like the Rothschilds and Sir Moses Montefiore to sponsor large-scale Jewish settlement. Though he died in 1874, before the Herzl era, Kalischer's writings helped lay the ideological foundation that would make modern Zionism possible.

Alkalai and Kalischer weren't inventing radical new ideas from thin air. They were rediscovering what the Hebrew prophets had written about extensively. The return of the Jewish people to their homeland from the four corners of the world is one of the most frequently repeated promise in the Hebrew Bible, described in great detail. Known in Hebrew as "Kibbutz Galuyot," the Ingathering of the Exiles, this return was mentioned by Moses in the Pentateuch in the 13th century BCE and restated by many of the Hebrew prophets spanning centuries, from Amos and Hosea who wrote in the 8th century BCE through Zechariah in the 5th century BCE.

Many of these ancient prophecies describe Israel's restoration unfolding in gradual stages, like natural processes. Isaiah (35:1–2) painted a picture of natural transformation, "The wilderness and the parched land shall be glad; the desert shall rejoice and blossom like a rose." Ezekiel (36:8) also described agricultural renewal, "But you, O mountains of Israel, you shall shoot forth your branches, and yield your fruit to My people Israel; for they are soon to come." According to the prophets themselves, redemption would be a natural process rather than a supernatural one. While obvious miracles might be clear signs of God's intentions, hidden miracles working through seemingly ordinary events carried even greater spiritual weight.

The prophets drew explicit contrasts between the original and supernaturally miraculous Exodus from Egypt and the future ingathering of the Jewish people. Micah (7:15) promised that the final redemption would mirror the first one: "As in the days when you came out of the land of Egypt, I will show them wonders." Yet Jeremiah (16:14–15) suggested it would actually overshadow the Exodus: "Therefore, behold, the days are coming, says the Lord, when it shall no longer be said, 'As the Lord lives, who brought up the children of Israel out of the land of Egypt,' but, 'As the Lord lives, who brought up the children of Israel from the land of the north and from all the lands where He had driven them.'"

How could anything overshadow the ten plagues of Egypt and the supernatural splitting of the Red Sea? The answer lay in the nature of the redemption itself. Unlike the Exodus, which happened in one dramatic fell swoop, the future redemption would be gradual and incremental. This would make it more real, more mature, and more permanent. After all, immediately following the miraculous Exodus, the Israelites began to complain and even begged to return to Egypt. The future redemption, unfolding slowly and naturally, would be lasting and eternal.

Alkalai and Kalischer were truly ahead of their times. Their writings were visionary, but living in small, isolated communities, they lacked the reach or platform to unite masses of Jews behind their ideas. The next generation would prove far more fertile ground for these revolutionary concepts.

Unlike his predecessors, who wrote in anticipation of future events, Rav Kook lived when Zionism had already become a mass movement complete with institutions, political parties, pioneering settlements, and intense conflicts between religious and secular Jews. Whereas his predecessors offered mainly practical arguments for Jewish settlement, Rav Kook developed a comprehensive spiritual worldview that gave cosmic meaning to the entire Zionist enterprise.

Finally, Kook differed from Alkalai and Kalischer on one crucial point that would prove historically decisive. They had naturally assumed that the settlers would be religiously observant Jews, whereas Rav Kook, who was living during the time of the Zionist pioneers, took the radical position that even secular, perhaps anti-religious, Jewish settlers were playing an essential role in God's redemptive plan.

Through his vast, mystical, and profound writings, Kook developed a theology of history. He bridged the seemingly unbridgeable gap between religious and secular Jews by presenting the secular Zionist pioneers as unconscious agents of redemption. This breakthrough developed an ideology of unity between traditionalists and innovators that proved to be indispensable for the creation of the State of Israel decades later. "We must not look down at our brethren who desecrate the Sabbath and appear as rebels," he wrote in his letters. "In truth, the spirit of the Lord is working through them to build and to plant... The profane will one day be sanctified."

Rav Kook was writing during a period of unprecedented change and gained credibility through real-life examples of unfolding events. As a result, his followers began to see everything that happened in regards to Palestine as infused with profound spiritual significance.

Portrait of Rabbi Abraham Isaac Kook (Photo by Zadok Basan)

When World War I broke out, Kook was visiting London and found himself stranded there for the duration of the conflict. Upon the announcement of the Balfour Declaration in 1917, Rav Kook was overwhelmed with gratitude to God, seeing it as a clear confirmation that world events were being orchestrated for the benefit of the restoration of the Jewish people. He viewed the war as a necessary step in the unfolding process of *Geulah* (redemption), with the collapse of old empires clearing the way for Jewish renewal.

Crucially, the theology of Religious Zionism, as shaped by Rav Kook, offered a fundamentally different approach to understanding Jewish messianic fulfillment. Where traditional discussions focused on distant future events to be revealed to a passive world at the End of Days, Rav Kook taught that the redemptive process was an ongoing historical reality in which all factions of the Jewish people actively participated. His thinking led to a remarkable embrace of diversity, especially for a traditional rabbi deeply immersed in Torah. "There is no extreme outlook that does not have a kernel of the truth," he wrote, finding value in capitalism, socialism, and even communism. Everything God created had a divine purpose and could be harnessed for God's ultimate plan.

Rav Kook's inclusive worldview led to some of the most touching scenes in early Zionist history. While the Second Aliyah pioneers were becoming increasingly distant from the Jewish traditions they left behind in Europe, the rabbinic community was digging its heels in and becoming increasingly opposed to Zionism. Rav Kook, on the other hand, regularly traveled around the country to farming communities whose members had rejected religious practice. He went out of his way to spend Sabbaths visiting anti-religious settlements, bringing his own kosher food but sharing meals and conversations with those who had abandoned the faith of their fathers. Here was a rabbi who could see divine sparks even in those who explicitly rejected religion, understanding their pioneering work as preparation for a spiritual awakening they themselves couldn't perceive.

Appreciating the return to Israel as an unfolding political process and recognizing spiritual meaning in contemporary events became defining characteristics of Religious Zionism. But Rav Kook went even further. In his eulogy for Theodor Herzl, the pious rabbi suggested that the secular founder of Political Zionism had played a role in human destiny far greater than anyone could have imagined.

When news of Herzl's death reached Jewish communities around the world in July of 1904, the response was unprecedented. From synagogues in Warsaw and London to the salons of Paris and Odessa, Jews who had never met the Zionist leader wept openly in the streets. The depth of this collective mourning revealed something remarkable. In just ten years, Thedor Herzl had transcended his role as a political leader to become something much greater in the Jewish imagination. But it was Rav Kook's eulogy delivered in Jerusalem that would revolutionize how the founder of Political Zionism was perceived.

Standing before the grieving crowd and drawing upon mystical Jewish sources, Kook gave a rabbinic discourse outlining two stages in the redemptive process. He spoke about the role of the Messiah in the redemption of Israel as embodied by, not one, but two Messiahs: Messiah the son of David and Messiah the son of Joseph. This concept of two messiahs existed in ancient Jewish wisdom, but it had remained largely obscure.

Rav Kook explained that the first phase of redemption would be led by Messiah son of Joseph, whose mission was to lay the groundwork for redemption through practical, material achievements. Like the biblical Joseph, who was a political statesman and whose acumen saved Egyptians from starving during the seven years of famine, Messiah son of Joseph would lay the material foundations for the restoration of Israel. However, this first messianic figure would not live to see the completion of his work. His role was to prepare the way for the second and final phase.

Only after the Messiah son of Joseph had completed his earthly mission and died would the Messiah son of David appear to bring the redemptive process to its spiritual fulfillment. This second messiah would transform not only the Jewish people but all of humanity, establishing the universal recognition of God and ushering in an era of unprecedented peace and harmony for the entire world.

Eulogizing Theodor Herzl, Rav Kook made an audacious declaration comparing the founder of Political Zionism to the Messiah son of Joseph, sending shockwaves through the Jewish world. "The soul of the Messiah son of Joseph appeared in him, to begin the redemption of Israel," said Rav Kook. "Even if he himself did not reach completion, through him the awakening of the redemption began."

With this eulogy, Rav Kook was elevating the spiritual significance of Political Zionism. The implications on Jewish thought were staggering. Jews, and especially the Torah observant community, should not only support secular Zionism, but should recognize it as an integral part of the messianic process itself, and opposition to Political Zionism was not just misguided but contrary to God's will.

Rav Kook's explanation of the two Messiahs is similar to the royal model based on King Saul and King David. Just as King Saul had built the political infrastructure and unified the kingdom to enable King David's spiritual renaissance, so too, the Messiah son of Joseph's material achievements would create the conditions for the Messiah son of David's spiritual transformation of the world. The body that Political Zionism was building would eventually receive the soul that Religious Zionism would provide.

This vision proved extraordinarily fruitful for the development of Zionism, as it provided a framework for unwavering religious support for Zionist institutions such as the government and the army. Rather than seeing the inevitable tension between secular and traditional Jews in Israeli life as a sign of failure, Religious Zionists could now understand that God's plan was for the reconciliation of contradictions. These ideological breakthroughs had the effect of infusing Zionism with spiritual energy for those who understood that their generation's primary mission was the achievement of Jewish unity in service to God.

While Rav Kook's breakthrough had the largest impact on Religious Zionists, his radical ideology reached many beyond his own community. The most unlikely person to embrace Rav Kook's messianic interpretation of Zionism was none other than David Ben-Gurion. Despite being avowedly secular and having little patience for religious observance, Ben-Gurion absorbed parts of Rav Kook's theological framework into his own outlook as the first Prime Minister of the Jewish state.

A SECULAR MESSIAH

After declaring independence in 1948, Ben-Gurion faced three overwhelming challenges that would have crushed a lesser leader. The War of Independence continued for over a year, requiring constant military mobilization and strategic planning. Simultaneously, Israel was absorbing immigration on a scale unprecedented in world history, doubling its population within three years through the arrival of Holocaust survivors and Jewish refugees from Arab countries. Finally, the new state had to create functioning governmental institutions from scratch while maintaining unity among Jewish communities that had been separated for centuries and often spoke different languages.

To Ben-Gurion, these challenges were not merely practical problems to be overcome, they were opportunities to infuse the new state with vision and purpose that would justify its existence to both its own citizens and the world. "There is no soul without a body," Ben-Gurion wrote in his book, *The Eternity of Israel*, "and no universal mission without national statehood." The state became Ben-Gurion's vehicle for crafting a body while making room for the soul. "The historical test of the Jewish people will not be in military force, the economy or the growth of the population, although these are all vital to its existence," Ben-

Gurion wrote in 1951. "That test will be in the mettle of its spirit, its vision, its prophetic and messianic mission."

For the secular Ben-Gurion, this "prophetic and messianic mission" was a deliberately chosen phrase. He understood the power of Jewish messianism in demonstrating that the Jews could create a society based on the highest moral principles. He envisioned Israel as a "light unto the nations," a biblical phrase that he understood in ethical rather than mystical terms encompassing civil liberties, equality before the law, and the national emancipation of the Jewish people within the family of nations. "Give honor to the State of Israel," he declared in one of his most famous speeches. "It is not merely an instrument for achieving independence. It is the beginning of the redemption."

To transform his vision into reality, Ben-Gurion championed a series of laws that would define Israel's soul and its identity as the nation-state of the Jewish people. The Law and Government Ordinance (1948) established Hebrew as the official language and recognized Jewish festivals as national holidays, ensuring that Israel's calendar and daily rhythm would reflect Jewish rather than Muslim traditions. The Flag and Emblem Law (1949) officially adopted symbols rooted in Jewish history, the blue and white flag echoing the colors of the *Tallit* prayer shawl, and the menorah emblem connecting modern Israel to the ancient Temple. The Law of Return (1950) granted every Jew around the world the right to immigrate to Israel and receive citizenship, emphasizing that Israel existed not just for its current residents but for the entire Jewish people. The Nationality Law (1952) formalized Israeli citizenship while maintaining special provisions for Jewish immigrants, and the State Education Law (1953) mandated that all Israeli children would receive education in Tanakh, Jewish history and Hebrew literature in the public school system.

Together, these laws created what Ben-Gurion called "public Judaism" – a shared Jewish identity that could unite secular and religious citizens around common symbols, memories, and aspirations. Ben-Gurion's most personal expression of public Judaism was his passion for biblical study. He studied the Hebrew Bible intensively, both privately and in public forums that captured national attention, such as the annual International Bible Contest that became a major cultural event, bringing together scholars from around the world to demonstrate their mastery of biblical knowledge. Through his Prime Minister's Bible Study Circle, Ben-Gurion brought together eminent Israeli biblical scholars for systematic study sessions every other Saturday at his Jerusalem home.

Ben-Gurion recognized that the Tanakh contained insights about human nature and social organization that no other ancient literature could match. He was particularly drawn to the Hebrew prophets' messianic ideal of universal justice and peace, seeing in their writings a blueprint for what the Jewish state could achieve. "We must indeed cultivate a messianic vision in Israeli youth," he declared, "and not merely a 'Zionist ideology.'" According to his biographer, "Ben-Gurion was not a religious man. His approach was always rigorously secular: the people had chosen and shaped its gods, and not God his people. His messianic vision had no religious significance but was invested with a concrete social-spiritual presence that called for constant elevation of society."

If Ben-Gurion did not believe in God or see the Messiah as the divine servant that Judaism envisioned, what was the source of his messianism? "My belief in this is based on recognition of the Jewish people and not on mystical faith," he explained in an article titled "In Defense of Messianism," where he articulated his views comprehensively. For Ben-Gurion, messianism meant the Jewish people's responsibility to demonstrate that a nation could be built on prophetic principles of justice, equality, and peace. Israel would fulfill its messianic mission not by waiting for divine intervention, but by creating a society so exemplary that other nations would seek to emulate its achievements. In his own secular way, Ben-Gurion was continuing the work that Rav Kook had begun and breathing a soul into the body that Political Zionism had created. He understood that a Jewish state without a Jewish soul would be nothing but a corpse.

The synthesis of Rav Kook's mystical vision with Ben-Gurion's practical statecraft created the ideological foundation that would shape Israel's soul for decades to come. Religious and secular Jews might disagree about theology, but they could unite around the shared idea that Israel represented something unprecedented in human history: a nation built on ancient wisdom while oriented toward universal redemption.

CENTRAL UNIVERSAL YESHIVA

Rav Kook's revolutionary ideas might have remained confined to academic circles were it not for his determination to train a new generation of religious leaders who could implement his vision. In 1924, he founded an unprecedented institution in Jerusalem that would become the intellectual powerhouse of Religious Zionism for generations to come.

Rav Kook named this seminary *haYeshiva haMerkazit haOlamit*, which he translated into English as "The Central Universal Yeshiva." In choosing this name, Rav Kook was crystallizing his revolutionary vision that would transform Zionism from an inward-looking Jewish nationalist movement into something far more expansive and world-embracing.

"*Yeshiva*" (seminary) anchored the institution in traditional European-style Jewish learning, demonstrating continuity with centuries of Torah scholarship. But "*Merkazit*" (central) broke new ground, signifying not merely an educational center but the institution's location in the spiritual epicenter of the world, Jerusalem. Most revolutionary was his choice of "*Olamit*" (universal), a term that captured Rav Kook's conviction that

Jewish renaissance in the Holy Land was never intended to benefit Jews alone. "*Olamit*" distinguished his vision from the defensive, insular approach of traditional European yeshivas that had turned inward during centuries of persecution. Instead, Rav Kook was proposing an outward-facing Judaism that would engage with humanity, absorb its best insights, and ultimately transform the entire world through Jewish spiritual renewal in the Land of Israel. Rav Kook's seminary would train rabbis who saw themselves not as guardians of an ancient tradition but as architects of a messianic future that would bless all of mankind.

The students of the Central Universal Yeshiva (better known as '*Mercaz*') understood that they were unique. They were the first generation of Torah scholars in nearly two millennia who weren't merely reading about biblical events from ancient texts; they were walking the same hills where Abraham had built altars, where David had composed psalms, and where the prophets had delivered their timeless messages. As they lived their daily lives in the Holy Land, they perceived themselves as writing the next chapters of the Tanakh.

This realization imbued Religious Zionism with a unique understanding of the Land of Israel itself. They saw the land as not merely national territory to be developed, but the covenantal promise that God had given to the Jewish people with divinely detailed boundaries recorded in Scripture. Where Political Zionism had focused on achieving normalcy among the nations, Religious Zionism taught that Israel was fundamentally different from all other territories, and therefore the Jewish people had certain sacred tasks unlike any other nation. Rav Kook's students demonstrated unprecedented devotion to settling the land with the rallying cry, *"Am Yisrael, b'Eretz Yisrael, al pi Torat Yisrael!"* meaning,"The Nation of Israel, in the Land of Israel, according to the Torah of Israel!"

Following Rav Kook's death in 1935, the leadership of Mercaz passed to his only son and intellectual heir, Rabbi Zvi Yehuda Kook (1891-1982). Whereas the father had been a mystic and philosopher whose writings soared through abstract theological concepts, the son proved to be a practical organizer and institution-builder who focused on systematizing his father's vision and transforming it into a concrete movement within Israeli society. Under Zvi Yehuda's dynamic leadership over nearly five decades, Religious Zionism expanded steadily throughout the country. Each generation of Israelis was becoming more traditional than the previous one, making Mercaz's influence increasingly significant year by year in all realms of Israeli life, from education and military service to politics and culture.

SIX DAYS OF WAR

Just as both World Wars had provided massive catalysts for the Zionist movement, the main transformation that elevated Religious Zionism from an intellectual stream into a dominant force in Israeli life came through the upheaval of the Six-Day War in June 1967.

The War of Independence ended with a cessation of hostilities, but not peace between Israel and her neighbors. As one Arab radio broadcast explained in June 1949, following the armistice agreement, "The Arabs will never cease to regard Israel as a hostile country. The Jews are our enemies...We do not pause for a single moment in our preparations for the day of vengeance." The Arabs' preparations took nearly two decades, and the day of vengeance finally came in May of 1967 when Egyptian President Gamal Abdel Nasser closed the Straits of Tiran to Israeli shipping.

This act of war was followed by Egypt expelling UN peacekeepers from the Sinai Desert, and mobilizing 100,000 soldiers along Israel's southern border. As the Arab armies of Egypt, Jordan, and Syria formed a military alliance and declared their intention to "wipe Israel off the map," the tiny Jewish state seemed to face imminent annihilation just twenty years after the Holocaust.

These were the dangerous days of the Cold War, and before Israel and America enjoyed a special relationship. While the Soviet Union supplied Arab armies with advanced weaponry, the United States maintained an arms embargo on Israel to avoid antagonizing the Soviets or disrupting the flow of Arab oil. Israel's strategic depth from east to west was a mere nine miles from the Jordanian-controlled mountains of Samaria to the Mediterranean Sea, making the Arab threat to "push the Jews into the sea" a terrifyingly realistic one. As Israel prepared for what seemed certain to be an existential battle, authorities ordered the grim task of digging mass graves in Tel Aviv's public parks to accommodate tens of thousands of anticipated civilian casualties. It was during these ominous days that Rabbi Zvi Yehuda Kook delivered his most powerful public remarks.

Speaking at Mercaz on Israeli Independence Day, May 15, 1967, Zvi Yehuda began by recalling the night in November 1947 when the United Nations had voted to partition British-controlled Palestine. Twenty years earlier, radios in all Jewish homes were tuned to the historic broadcast from New York. And when the outcome of the vote was announced, and the UN voted in favor of partitioning a Jewish state and an Arab state, spontaneous celebrations erupted in the streets throughout Jewish Palestine. But as Zvi Yehuda revealed to his Mercaz students, he had experienced that momentous night very differently. The memory still overwhelmed him with emotion, and his voice broke as he recalled his anguish.

"I couldn't leave the house that night," he confessed. "I was so heartbroken. I couldn't go out to join the festive celebrations on Jaffa Street. I sat alone. Distressed. It weighed so heavily on me. In those first hours, I couldn't come to terms with what had happened. The word of God had come to pass, 'They have divided My Land!' (Joel 4:2)."

Then, with an intensity that electrified everyone present, Rabbi Zvi Yehuda shouted at the top of his lungs:

"WHERE IS OUR HEBRON?! DID WE FORGET?! WHERE IS OUR SHECHEM?! DO WE FORGET ABOUT THIS?! WHERE IS OUR JERICHO?! DO WE FORGET THIS, TOO?! WHERE IS EACH PARCEL OF GOD'S LAND?!"

Hebron, Shechem and Jericho were important biblical cities that had been lost by Israel during the War of Independence and remained under Jordanian occupation, separated by barbed wire and minefields.

His students had gathered to celebrate independence that evening in May 1967, but Rabbi Zvi Yehuda wanted them to understand that their sovereignty remained tragically incomplete while the biblical heartland remained occupied by hostile Arabs. Yet, just three weeks after his heartbroken speech, his lament was overturned.

On the morning of June 5, Israel launched a preemptive attack. Wave after wave of Israeli Air Force jets struck Egyptian targets and effectively incapacitated Egypt within hours. Egypt took to the airwaves and, in order to trick their Syrian and Jordanian allies into attacking Israel, lied on Arabic radio that Egyptian forces were destroying Tel Aviv. Despite Israeli warnings to Jordan's King Hussein not to get involved, Jordanian forces started shelling Jewish Jerusalem from the east. Syria and Iraq attacked Israel from the north, and Israel found itself fighting simultaneously on all of its borders.

In less than a week, Israel went from digging mass graves to achieving a military victory so stunning it could only be explained as the hand of God. When the Six-Day War finally concluded on June 11, the outcome exceeded even the most optimistic Israeli expectations. The country had captured territories nearly tripling its size, including the biblical cities of Hebron, Shechem, Jericho, and Jerusalem.

IDF Paratroopers at the Western Wall during the Six Day War (Photo by David Rubinger, June 1967)

The IDF had been so preoccupied with defending their small state that they hadn't even drawn up plans to capture Jerusalem's Old City and lacked accurate maps to help soldiers navigate the narrow alleys with their jeeps. Yet by June 7, Jewish forces had reached the Temple Mount and the Western Wall, Judaism's holiest sites that had been inaccessible to Jews for nineteen years. One of the first Israeli soldiers to reach the Temple Mount was Yisrael Ariel, a Mercaz student serving as a paratrooper. He was there for the historic moment when IDF Chief of Staff General Mordechai "Motta" Gur announced over the radio, "The Temple Mount is in our hands!"

"As we ascended the Temple Mount, I saw two soldiers running into the Dome of the Rock, and I was in shock... They raised the Israeli flag on the mosque, and I thought to myself, 'This is a different world we live in today than yesterday.' From atop the mount, looking down at the Western Wall, I saw two elderly men dressed in white moving about near the wall below. I couldn't believe my eyes. At that moment, I thought these men were Elijah the Prophet along with the King Messiah himself.'"

The enthusiastic Religious Zionist response to these extraordinary developments was immediate. Three months after the Six-Day War, a young Mercaz student, Chanan Porat, led a group of Israeli families to begin settling the newly captured territory known by its biblical name of Judea and Samaria. For Porat, it was personal. He was born in a town south of Jerusalem known as Kfar Etzion in 1943. The small Jewish community was surrounded by larger Arab towns, and during the War of Independence, the IDF didn't have enough manpower to properly defend the area. Porat, who was five years old at the time, was evacuated with the women and children to Jerusalem, while the men stayed to defend their community, including his own father.

On May 13, 1948, the day before Ben-Gurion would declare the birth of the State, Arab local fighters launched a brutal assault on Kfar Etzion. Outnumbered and outgunned, the courageous defenders fought with everything they had, holding off wave after wave of Arab soldiers. By evening, the 130 Israeli men ran out of ammunition and surrendered, only to be massacred by the Arab forces. And so, when Chanan Porat returned in September 1967 to Kfar Etzion, he was returning as a 24-year-old to rebuild his home on the very ground where his father had died defending his community. Kfar Etzion was the first Jewish settlement to be built in Judea and Samaria, and a powerful symbol of the Religious

Zionist settlement movement. The pioneers saw themselves as the living embodiment of what the prophet Isaiah had promised, "Your people shall rebuild the ancient ruins; you shall raise up the foundations of many generations" (Isaiah 58:12).

The following spring, Religious Zionist students led another pioneering effort, this time to the heart of Hebron. A group of young Israeli women arrived to celebrate Passover in Hebron, the ancient city where the patriarchs and matriarchs are buried. They rented a building called Beit Hadassah from local Arabs, which had been the city's Jewish hospital before 1929. When Israeli authorities tried to remove them after the holiday, the women refused to leave, declaring that Jews had a right to live in the city of their matriarchs and patriarchs. Their courageous stand established the first permanent Jewish presence in Hebron since the 1929 massacre that had driven out the ancient Jewish community.

Similar stories unfolded throughout the biblical heartland as Jewish pioneers returned to places that had sustained Jewish dreams throughout two millennia of exile. They resettled Shiloh, where the Tabernacle had rested for 369 years and where Hannah had prayed for a son. They returned to Bethel, where Jacob had dreamed of a ladder ascending to the heavens. They established communities on Mount Gerizim, the hill where the Israelites had gathered to receive blessings. They built homes in Bethlehem, where Rachel was buried and in Jericho, which Joshua had conquered after marching around the city seven times.

These settlement efforts evolved into the Gush Emunim (Bloc of the Faithful) movement, characterized by remarkable persistence and creativity. With often tacit support from Israel's left-wing Labor government under Prime Minister Yitzhak Rabin, who understood that these communities strengthened Israel's security position, Gush Emunim families established Jewish settlements throughout Judea and Samaria. The strategic importance was undeniable: these territories lie on a mountain range overlooking Israel's coastal plain, and control of the region provides essential defensive depth for Israel's largest cities.

Religious Zionists were determined to establish a permanent Jewish presence in the newly liberated biblical heartland, fulfilling the divine promises that had sustained the Jewish people throughout their long exile. As the prophet Jeremiah had foretold, "Your children have returned to their border" (Jeremiah 31:17). What began as spontaneous responses to the miraculous victory of 1967 would soon evolve into the organized settlement movement that would define Religious Zionism for generations to come.

Jews from around the world resettled the towns of Judea and Samaria, and the land responded to the return of its children in remarkable ways. Even though the terrain was rocky and seemingly barren, the hilltops were lovingly tended by Israeli settlers. Reading in their Bibles about the ancient "vineyards of Samaria," Jewish farmers began planting grapes despite professional advice that it was impossible. Yet in just a few short years, with hard work and divine blessing, some of those vineyards produced award-winning wines and bottles of liquid prophecy.

Beyond the agricultural miracles they were performing, Religious Zionists established new schools and yeshivot throughout Judea and Samaria, educating the next generation of idealistic and patriotic students. These institutions became fertile grounds for some of Israel's most motivated soldiers, with knit-kippa-wearing youth filling the ranks of elite IDF units, gradually replacing the secular kibbutzim as the primary source of Israel's most dedicated military leaders.

BILLY GRAHAM'S BLOCKBUSTER

Religious Zionists gradually extended their influence across every sphere of Israeli life - from business and politics to culture and education. Their use of biblical language and their visible, deep-rooted faith resonated strongly with Christian Zionists worldwide. For more than a century, these Christians had viewed Israel through a biblical lens, but now they watched with awe as Israel's restoration unfolded, inspiring them with renewed spiritual fervor to strengthen their own bond with the Jewish state.

Israel's awe-inspiring victory in the Six-Day War was a turning point not only in Jewish history but also in the way Evangelical Christians around the world related to the modern State of Israel. Into this moment of spiritual and political awakening stepped the Billy Graham Evangelistic Association with its 1970 film *His Land*. The movie took the evangelical world by storm and was shown to millions of churchgoers. For Christians, *His Land* visually and emotionally connected biblical prophecy to the contemporary rebirth of Israel, helping Christians see the Jewish state not as a distant foreign nation but as part of their own sacred story.

Remarkably, the film was embraced by Jewish organizations as well, including the American Jewish Committee, which organized screenings in synagogues despite its clear evangelical agenda. This unprecedented cooperation signaled a dramatic shift in Jewish-Christian relations, showing that evangelical enthusiasm for Israel could be framed in ways that Jews found respectful and supportive. *His Land* helped create a cultural bridge between the prophetic excitement unleashed by the Six-Day War and the political mobilization of Christian Zionism that would emerge in the following decade.

While the Six-Day War invigorated Christian Zionism, the movement itself wasn't entirely new and had been evolving for generations. Christians who supported the restoration of the Jews to Israel had been part of America's story since the early days of the Republic. President John Adams wrote to a Jewish acquaintance, "I could find it in my heart to wish that you had been at the head of a hundred thousand Israelites... and marching with them into Judea and making a conquest of that country and restoring your nation to the dominion of it. For I really wish the Jews again in Judea an independent nation."

Christians did far more than wish the Jews well in becoming an independent nation. Their activism on behalf of Jewish restoration predated Theodor Herzl by decades, and they actively took steps to develop the land, seeing their role as gentile facilitators explicitly prescribed in Scripture.

George Bush (1796–1859), ancestor of two American presidents who would bear the same name, was a pioneering biblical scholar, Hebraist, and early Christian Zionist whose work significantly influenced 19th-century American religious thought. A Presbyterian minister who became professor of Hebrew at New York University in 1831, Bush championed Jewish restoration with scholarly rigor and prophetic passion.

In 1844, Bush published *The Dry Bones of Israel Revived*, arguing that the restoration of the Jewish people to their ancestral homeland would elevate not only the Jews but all of humanity, forming a "link of communication between humanity and God." Drawing from Ezekiel 37's vision of dry bones coming to life, Bush grounded his theology in explicit biblical commands that assigned gentiles an active role in Jewish restoration.

Isaiah (49:22) particularly captivated Christian Zionists: "Thus said my Sovereign God: I will raise My hand to nations and lift up My ensign to peoples; and they shall bring your sons in their bosoms, and carry your daughters on their backs." This passage didn't merely predict Jewish return - it commanded the nations to assist in bringing Jews back to the Land of Israel.

But the prophetic mandate extended beyond immigration. Isaiah envisioned gentiles actively participating in the land's revitalization: "And they shall build the ancient ruins, raise up the desolations of old, and renew the ruined cities, the desolations of many ages. Strangers shall stand and pasture your flocks, aliens shall be your plowers and vine-trimmers" (Isaiah 61:4-5).

Taking these prophecies as divine marching orders, Christian missionaries from across the world began arriving in the Holy Land throughout the 19th century. They established hospitals and schools that served both Jewish and Arab populations, providing essential infrastructure in a neglected Ottoman backwater.

These Christian pioneers also revolutionized biblical archaeology, transforming it from treasure hunting into scientific discipline. Scholars like Edward Robinson and William Foxwell Albright were among the first to systematically excavate sites such as the City of David and other crucial locations, providing tangible proof of the ancient connection between the Jewish people, their land, and their Book. Their discoveries would later provide powerful evidence for Zionist claims to indigenous status in Palestine.

These early examples of Christian Zionism demonstrated that support for Jewish restoration was deeply rooted in biblical theology. Yet it wasn't until the twin events of the Holocaust and the establishment of the State of Israel that the relationship between Christians and Jews would be truly and profoundly reshaped the way Christians perceived Jews - and how Jews, in turn, viewed Christians.

Rabbi Joseph B. Soloveitchik, one of American Jewry's foremost thinkers, observed in 1961 that "the establishment of the State of

Israel has publicly refuted all the claims of Christian theologians who argued that God had stripped the Jewish people of its rights to the Land of Israel, and that the biblical promises concerning Zion and Jerusalem referred only, in allegorical fashion, to Christianity."

What Rabbi Soloveitchik was observing was the beginning of Christianity's rejection of one of its most destructive theological foundations - Replacement Theology, the root cause of centuries of antisemitic persecution.

THE POISON OF REPLACEMENT THEOLOGY

Ever since Christianity emerged as an outgrowth of first-century Judaism, it engaged in theological conflict with its parent faith. While Jesus and the apostles were Jews living in Israel who did not see themselves as starting a new religion, some of the early church fathers, in their effort to distinguish Christianity from its Jewish origins, embraced a harsh theology that attacked the faith of Jesus himself with a vengeance.

Replacement Theology, also known as Supersessionism, taught that because the Jewish people rejected Jesus as the Messiah, God punished them by annulling His covenant and transferring His promises to the Church. According to this doctrine, the Church became the "New Israel," inheriting all of God's blessings, while the Jews were left with His curses. This theology supplied a powerful religious rationale for portraying Jews as condemned and for justifying their persecution, marginalization, and even elimination.

The practical consequences of Replacement Theology were catastrophic for Jewish communities throughout Christian Europe. During the Crusades of the 11th and 12th centuries, Christian armies aimed to liberate the Holy Land from Muslim control, but massacred "infidel" Jews along their route, viewing them as enemies of Christ who deserved death. Throughout medieval Christian Europe, Jews were frequently forced to choose between conversion to Christianity or expulsion from their homes and countries. During the Spanish Inquisition, even Jewish converts to Christianity were subjected to brutal torture to test whether their conversions were genuine.

Martin Luther, the 16th-century Protestant reformer who broke from Roman Catholicism, initially hoped that Jews would embrace his "purified" form of Christianity. When they did not, he turned against them with a fury, penning virulently antisemitic treatises that centuries later were cited approvingly by Nazi propagandists. Over the generations, Jews were repeatedly accused in baseless "Blood Libel" cases of murdering Christian children, and they faced brutal pogroms, expulsions, and systemic discrimination wherever they lived. These attacks were not isolated incidents but part of a continuous tradition of Christian antisemitism that embedded hatred into European culture. That centuries-long hostility ultimately culminated in the Holocaust, where six million Jews were annihilated, often with the active encouragement or silent complicity of Christian leaders, churches, and lay populations across the continent.

The encounter between Theodor Herzl and Pope Pius X in 1904 illustrates how Replacement Theology made Christian support for Jewish restoration impossible. After years of trying to arrange the meeting, Herzl finally gained an audience with the most powerful religious leader in the world to plead the case of the Jewish people. Herzl explained the Jewish yearning for a homeland after centuries of exile and persecution.

The Pope categorically dismissed Herzl's request, "We cannot prevent the Jews from going to Jerusalem, but we can never sanction it. The Jews have not recognized our Lord; therefore, we cannot recognize the Jewish people. And so, if you come to Palestine and settle your people there, we will be ready with churches and priests to baptize them." For Pope Pius X, as for centuries of Christian thinkers, Jewish restoration without Christian conversion was theologically impossible. God's promises now belonged to the church, not to the Jews who had supposedly forfeited them by rejecting Jesus.

While Replacement Theology brought immense suffering upon the Jewish people, its consequences were even more devastating for Christianity itself and for the moral fabric of the world. The ingathering of Israel to its land is not a marginal biblical theme but the single most repeated promise in all of Scripture. Every Hebrew prophet, without exception, proclaimed Israel's restoration as a central pillar of God's redemptive plan for humanity. To oppose or obstruct this divine design is not merely sacrilegious - it is perilous. As the prophet Zechariah declared: "Whoever touches you touches the apple of His eye" (Zechariah 2:8).

Christian Europe's attempt to usurp Israel's role created a spiritual sickness that manifested in unprecedented evil. When a religion makes it an official policy to obstruct God's plan, it opens the door to moral catastrophe. It is thus no surprise that Europe - the continent that embraced Replacement Theology most fervently - became the birthplace and breeding ground of history's greatest horrors. Only after the devastation of the Holocaust and the miraculous success of the State of Israel did significant numbers of Christians begin to question the veracity of Replacement Theology.

American Christian theologians such as Reinhold Niebuhr argued that centuries of church hostility toward Jews had helped create the cultural climate in which Nazism could take root. Niebuhr himself became an outspoken supporter of the State of Israel, recognizing it as part of Christianity's moral responsibility toward the Jewish people. In the aftermath of the Holocaust, Christian councils across the United States were compelled to confront the legacy of antisemitism and began taking new steps to build bridges with the Jewish community.

Although many Jewish leaders remained skeptical of Christian outreach, Israeli Prime Ministers Golda Meir and Menachem Begin cultivated relationships with American Christian leaders, including Billy Graham, Jerry Falwell, and Pat Robertson. Each of these influential figures utilized their massive platforms to publicly support Israel and began promoting a theology of Christian Zionism that reversed centuries of Replacement Theology.

In massive gatherings held in stadiums around the world, Billy Graham preached that God kept His eternal covenant with Israel. "The Jews are God's chosen people," Graham declared. "We cannot place ourselves in opposition to Israel without detriment to ourselves."

Televangelist Pat Robertson articulated on his hugely popular "700 Club" television program that rather than being replaced, Israel's success is evidence of biblical truth and that in no way was Christianity in opposition to Judaism:

> "You must realize that the God who spoke to Moses on Mount Sinai is our God. Abraham, Isaac, and Jacob are our spiritual Patriarchs. Jeremiah, Ezekiel, and Daniel are our prophets. King David, a man after God's own heart, is our hero. The Holy City of Jerusalem is our spiritual capital. And the continuation of Jewish sovereignty over the Holy Land is a further bulwark to us that the God of the Bible exists and that His Word is true."

Jerry Falwell, one of the most prominent evangelical leaders of the 20th century, was another unwavering supporter of Israel. Through his political movement, the Moral Majority, he framed solidarity with the Jewish state as both a biblical obligation and a matter of American national interest. Falwell argued that America's prosperity in the modern era was, in part, a divine reward for standing with Israel. On Capitol Hill, he reminded lawmakers that "history supports the premise that God deals with nations as they deal with Israel," citing God's promise to Abraham in Genesis 12:3: "I will bless those who bless you."

In the decades following the Six-Day War, churches across the American Bible Belt began raising Israeli flags alongside the Stars and Stripes. Pastors wove calls to support Israel into their sermons, and Christian voters demanded that their representatives uphold a strong pro-Israel stance. This groundswell of Christian solidarity with the Jewish return to their land stands as a remarkable miracle - one still not fully grasped by many Jews. The very nations and communities that had long persecuted God's chosen people were now emerging as some of their staunchest advocates. This dramatic reversal recalls the prophecy of Isaiah (60:14): "The children of your oppressors will come bowing before you; all who despised you will bow down at your feet and will call you the City of the Lord, Zion of the Holy One of Israel."

The turning of Gentile nations toward Israel marks another significant milestone in the unfolding redemption process, as understood by Religious Zionism. Scripture suggests that God's miracles on behalf of Israel will first be recognized by the nations of the world, even before they are fully acknowledged by the Jewish people themselves. Psalm 126 vividly captures this vision of restoration: "When the Lord restored the fortunes of Zion, we were like dreamers. Then our mouth was filled with laughter, and our tongue with songs of joy. Then it was said among the nations, 'The Lord has done great things for them.' The Lord has done great things for us, and we rejoiced."

The psalm's progression is revealing. First comes Israel's restoration, then the nations recognize what God has accomplished, and finally this gentile recognition serves to encourage the Jewish people themselves. Jews recite Psalm 126 frequently as part of the Grace After Meals, yet most are probably unaware that Christian Zionism might represent the fulfillment of this ancient prophecy.

CHALLENGES OF LAND FOR PEACE

In the decade following the Six-Day War, Israel found itself at the center of an international debate over the future of the territories it had captured. The war left Israel in control of vast new areas: the oil-rich Sinai Peninsula, the strategically vital Golan Heights, the Gaza Strip, and the biblical heartland of Judea and Samaria. While Israel annexed East Jerusalem and formally declared its sovereignty there, it refrained from doing the same with the other territories. Instead, Israel established a system of military administration, in which the IDF maintained security while local Arab communities continued to govern their own civilian affairs.

During the 1970s and 1980s, Religious Zionism gave birth to the modern settlement movement, as its leaders and followers, driven by deep faith and an unshakable belief in the eternal bond between the Jewish people and their land, began establishing new communities across Judea and Samaria. Their momentum, however, eventually faced a significant ideological setback as growing international pressure mounted on Israel to relinquish territories captured in 1967 in exchange for the promise of "Land for Peace" with its Arab neighbors.

The first major phase of "Land for Peace" came with Egyptian President Anwar Sadat's dramatic visit to Jerusalem in 1977, which led to the signing of the Camp David Accords in 1978. In exchange for a peace treaty with Egypt, Israel agreed to return the entire Sinai Peninsula, including its oil fields and the thriving new Israeli city of Yamit. In 1982, thousands of Israeli settlers were forcibly evacuated from their homes in Sinai, creating traumatic scenes as Israeli soldiers removed Jewish families from communities they had built with their own hands.

The Palestinian situation proved even more complex. After years of Palestinian terrorism, Israeli leaders became so desperate for peace and quiet that they offered to withdraw from nearly all of Judea and Samaria (known also as the West Bank) through an agreement they secretly negotiated with Palestinian leaders in Oslo. Although many Israelis were horrified by the notion of granting autonomy and weapons to the Arabs, the Land for Peace movement had grown in momentum. The sight of Prime Minister Yitzhak Rabin shaking hands with PLO leader Yasser Arafat on the White House lawn in September 1993, under the watchful eye of President Bill Clinton, seemed to herald a new era of peace and coexistence.

Prime Minister of Israel, Yitzhak Rabin, US President Bill Clinton, and PLO chairman Yasser Arafat at the White House (Photo by GPO, September 1993)

Successive Israeli governments found themselves offering more and more land for less and less peace. With each Israeli concession,

Palestinian terrorism increased, and many Israelis became convinced that separation, rather than integration, offered the only path to security. This philosophy reached its climax in 2005 when Prime Minister Ariel Sharon, a longtime champion of the settlement movement, led the "Disengagement" - a unilateral Israeli withdrawal from the Gaza Strip.

More than 8,000 Israelis were forcibly removed from 21 thriving communities in Gaza that together formed Gush Katif, where Jewish farmers had turned barren sand dunes into some of the most productive agricultural land in the region. Many of these families had lived there for decades, building prosperous towns and playing a vital role in Israel's security by serving as a buffer against the growing threat of radicalized jihadist Arabs in the Gaza Strip.

The Disengagement proved to be both a strategic disaster for Israel and a profound crisis of faith for the Religious Zionist community. It shook their core convictions about divine providence and the unfolding redemption. The vision of Rav Kook - that the gradual settlement of the Land of Israel would pave the way toward messianic fulfillment - seemed to be contradicted by this dramatic reversal. If God was truly guiding Jewish restoration, how could devoted Jews be expelled from their ancestral homeland by their own government?

Beyond the material loss of abandoning homes, synagogues, and thriving businesses, the Disengagement left a deep emotional and spiritual scar across Israel. The pain was compounded in the very moment the last Israelis departed Gush Katif, when Palestinian Arabs entered - not to preserve and inhabit the flourishing communities that had been handed over - but to torch the houses and synagogues and to tear apart the greenhouses with their bare hands, erasing years of labor and hope in a matter of days.

Why would anyone moving into a new neighborhood destroy perfectly functional homes and agricultural infrastructure that could provide food and shelter? The answer lies in the same destructive impulse that drove the ancient Philistines to block the wells that Abraham and Isaac had dug, as recorded in Genesis.

Isaac prospered greatly in Gerar, near present-day Gaza, under Abimelech, king of the Philistines. His fields produced a hundredfold and his flocks multiplied, arousing the envy of his neighbors. As he retraced the journey of his father Abraham, Isaac reopened ancient wells, only to find many of them deliberately stopped up. As Genesis (26:15) records: "All the wells that his father's servants had dug in the days of Abraham his father, the Philistines stopped them and filled them with earth." In the ancient world, destroying wells meant cutting off life itself - an act of hatred that helped no one. This same impulse can be seen in modern Palestinian rejectionism: the choice to destroy rather than build, to embrace ruin instead of the prosperity that could serve all. Spiritually, Gaza has long stood as a symbol of resistance to God's plan for Israel's restoration.

Sharon's withdrawal from Gaza was supposed to enhance Israeli security while demonstrating to the world Israel's commitment to peace. Instead, the terror group Hamas immediately seized control of the territory. They murdered anyone who stood in their way and abrogated all previous Palestinian commitments to peaceful coexistence, establishing a despotic regime built on terror and oppression. From their new base in Gaza, Hamas turned its weapons against Israel, launching thousands of rockets at civilian population centers. What was supposed to bring peace instead created a frontline of terror on Israel's southern border.

Instead of recognizing their mistake and responding with force, successive Israeli governments built the Iron Dome missile defense system to intercept Hamas rockets. But this defensive posture only emboldened Hamas. Rather than building infrastructure for their citizens, they constructed an elaborate network of tunnels beneath Gaza, both to infiltrate Israel and to hide their growing arsenal of weapons. In the years following their takeover in 2006, Hamas transformed the Gaza Strip into a massive terror base dedicated to Israel's destruction. The true cost of that reality became horrifically clear on October 7th, 2023, when Hamas unleashed the full force of the nightmare it had been preparing for two decades.

On that terrible morning, Hamas terrorists and Gazan civilians emerged from their tunnels to launch a coordinated surprise attack years in the making. Firing thousands of rockets into Israel, Hamas terrorists overwhelmed IDF border positions and poured into Israeli border communities. They murdered entire families, raped women, beheaded men, killed children in front of their parents, slaughtered hundreds of young people at a music festival, and dragged over 250 hostages back into Gaza's tunnels.

The brutal horror of the October 7th attack confirmed what many Religious Zionists had been warning for years: only Jewish settlement leads to peace, while surrendering land brings more war. Yet from the terrifying darkness, a new understanding is beginning to take shape. At the core of Religious Zionist faith is the conviction that every setback contains the seed of greater growth - that from darkness, great light will emerge. The role of evil in the world is to strike at the good, forcing it to rise with a strength it could never have found otherwise.

After the Disengagement from Gaza, the settlement ideal that had inspired thousands of pioneering families suddenly appeared to be a wasted effort and even a lost cause. The Religious Zionist movement, which had been gaining strength and influence for decades, was left shaken, divided, and demoralized. Yet the failure of the "Land for Peace" formula has since made clear that neither security nor spiritual fulfillment can be achieved by retreating from Israel's mission in the world. The horrors of October 7th have now created the conditions for Rav Kook's vision to reach far beyond its original base, finding new resonance across Israeli society.

For the first time, many secular Israelis are recognizing that the settlements in Judea and Samaria, populated by idealistic religious families and long portrayed as controversial obstacles to peace, actually serve as Israel's first line of defense. Many are beginning to appreciate the incredible dedication and sacrifices made by the Religious Zionist community, who not only settled Judea and Samaria at great personal risk but also paid a disproportionately high share of the war effort. Although Religious Zionists comprise about 10% of the Israeli population, approximately 50% of the IDF soldiers killed or wounded in the war following October 7 were Religious Zionists. The rest of the country has begun to realize that there is not a single Religious Zionist school, neighborhood, or yeshiva that has not suffered the loss of a soldier - whether fallen or wounded.

That recognition has inspired genuine admiration. Israeli soldiers fighting on multiple fronts witnessed their religiously observant comrades holding fast to daily Torah study and prayer even under the most exhausting conditions. For the first time, many secular Israelis began to see religious faith not as a weakness but as a source of strength. Across the military, this sparked the beginnings of a religious revival.

When the war broke out over the Simchat Torah holiday, soldiers were called up and immediately reported for duty without having any time to prepare or pack. In the early days of the war, the most requested item from IDF soldiers was not food or other basic necessities they didn't have time to pack, but *tzitzit* - the ritual fringes commanded by the Torah and worn by observant Jewish men. Across Israel, religious students worked around the clock hand-stitching camouflage-colored *tzitzit* to send to the front lines, where secular soldiers asked to wear them for spiritual protection.

Countless videos spread across Israeli social media showing secular soldiers praying and keeping Shabbat. This was not coerced religiosity, but a genuine awakening to spiritual resources that their secular upbringing had never offered. When these soldiers rotated home from the front, they carried with them a new perspective - one that cut through the ideological divides that had long fractured Israeli society.

This was no coincidence. David Ben-Gurion understood the important role the IDF would play in unifying Israeli society and elevating Jewish identity. "I see in the military not only the fortress that secures us, although this would be sufficient," he explained, "but also an educational force for raising up the Jewish man, a cement for bringing together the nation, and a faithful mechanism for the absorption of immigrants."

Hostage families embraced prayer and Shabbat observance, finding comfort in ancient traditions. Government officials from Netanyahu down peppered their speeches with appeals for divine help and thanksgiving for revealed miracles. October 7th triggered not only military mobilization but religious revival throughout Israel.

In cramped tanks in the north and the south, Israeli soldiers served alongside others from every background: Ashkenazi and Sephardi, religious and secular, left and right, from major cities and small settlements. Israelis began to recognize what Rav Kook taught one hundred years ago: that their diversity is not a weakness to be smoothed over, but rather the very source of their strength.

CHILDREN LEADING THEIR PARENTS

Rav Kook envisioned a movement that embraced all Jews. Sadly, it took a terrible war, but finally, Israeli society is becoming more cohesive and unified. Remarkably, the Biblical values of Religious

Zionism are beginning to spread outwards, not from the top down, but from the bottom up. Not from the parents to their children, but from the younger generation to the rest of society.

> "Behold, I will send you Elijah the prophet before the coming of the great and awesome day of the Lord. And he will turn the heart of the fathers to the children, and the heart of the children to their fathers." (Malachi 3:23-24)

These words, written over 2,400 years ago, illuminate our current moment. The prophet Malachi lived during the Second Temple period, after the Jewish people returned from Babylonian exile, a time of both physical and spiritual rebuilding. At first glance, Malachi's prophecy seems backwards. Throughout history, older generations have typically possessed greater wisdom and moral authority than their children. It would therefore be natural that before the arrival of Elijah, the harbinger of the messianic era, the hearts of children would first turn toward their parents.

Yet Malachi's formulation suggests the opposite. "Before the coming of the great and awesome day of the Lord," the younger generation will possess something special that their parents lack, something so significant that it will inspire the older generation to follow their children's lead. The prophet envisions a time when moral clarity and spiritual courage will flow upward from young to old, when the next generation will show their parents the path forward.

That time has arrived in Israel today. The 300,000 Israeli soldiers who enlisted following October 7th represent something unprecedented in modern Israeli history. With enlistment rates in many units surpassing 100% - as more men and women reported for duty than were even summoned - young Israelis have shown a devotion to their people and their land that rises above the political divisions which had long paralyzed their parents.

Before the war, many observers dismissed Israeli Gen Z and millennials as the "TikTok generation." They were criticized for their absorption in social media and apparent disconnection from the grand narratives that shaped previous generations who built the country. Yet when their nation needed them, they set aside their phones, abandoned their comfortable lives, and rushed to defend their brothers and sisters.

On perhaps the most consequential day of the war, just hours before Israel carried out a dramatic series of strikes on Iranian nuclear and missile targets, Prime Minister Netanyahu visited the Western Wall. He placed a note of prayer into the Wall bearing a biblical verse: "A people that rises up as a lioness, and as a lion lifts himself up." The symbolic gesture and mysterious note came ahead of what Netanyahu later described as a "very successful opening strike" under a new military campaign - Operation Rising Lion.

This current generation of Rising Lions represents the finest the Jewish people have ever produced in our long history. The divisions that plagued previous generations of Israelis are dissolving as a new sense of spiritual purpose emerges. To understand the magnitude of this transformation, we must recognize what these young people are leaving behind. Their shift from defense to purpose marks a fundamental break from the past.

For decades, Jews lived with a siege mentality, surrounded by enemies and forced to focus primarily on survival. This defensive posture created a society that was primarily reactive rather than proactive, more focused on avoiding attacks than on achieving greatness. In recent years especially, Israelis struggled to articulate a compelling vision of what they were building toward rather than what they were defending against.

As Malachi prophesied, the hearts of parents are turning toward their children, recognizing that this younger generation has reclaimed something precious their elders had lost: the confidence that comes from moral clarity, the strength that flows from spiritual purpose, and the unity forged through shared sacrifice. Having proven their ability to fight, the generation of Rising Lions is now developing a mission mentality - and they have earned the right to dream about what comes next for Israel and the world.

This unity of purpose, powerful as it is, must serve a purpose beyond physical survival. The Torah refers to the Jewish people as "*beni bechori Yisrael*" - "My firstborn son, Israel" (Exodus 4:22). Like any firstborn, the Jewish people carry a unique burden and responsibility. Just as no parent wants to see their children fighting among themselves, God desires unity among His people as the foundation for fulfilling their sacred mission.

Only through drawing closer to each other and to God in unity, can the Jewish people be spiritually prepared to advance to the next stage. Then, unified in service to God and in observance of His Torah, Israel can effectively reach outward to bless the nations. A house divided, a people distant from their Creator, cannot stand as a light unto the nations. The unity emerging from October 7th's crucible is not merely about Jewish survival - it's about preparing the Jewish people, through repentance and Torah observance, to fulfill their ancient covenant as a "kingdom of priests and a holy nation" (Exodus 19:6).

While October 7th was the worst national crisis facing the Jewish people in recent memory, the first great national crisis was the destruction of the Temple in Jerusalem. The Talmud examines what led to that catastrophe and arrives at a striking conclusion - rather than blaming Israel's enemies, it identifies the internal sin of baseless hatred as the cause of lost sovereignty. Rav Kook drew a profound lesson from this: if the Temple was destroyed through *Sinat Chinam* (baseless hatred), it can only be rebuilt through

Ahavat Chinam (baseless love) - radical unity and internal cohesion that transcends all divisions.

The generation of Rising Lions which has demonstrated such great unity of purpose can begin to lead the rest of the nation towards the next phase of Zionism. However, unity achieved through facing a common enemy is only temporary. October 7th reminded us that we share external enemies but have not yet defined our internal purpose. It brought tremendous solidarity, but not necessarily lasting unification.

For there to be true and enduring unity in Israel, a precondition for national restoration, the source of our unity must be a grand mission and transformative idea.

That grand mission and transformative idea is Universal Zionism.

UNIVERSAL ZIONISM

4

UNIVERSAL ZIONISM

Solomon's succession to his father's throne was anything but inevitable. As King David lay dying, his son Adonijah declared himself king - and the old warrior did nothing to stop him. David's passivity revealed a pattern that runs throughout Scripture: Abraham tolerated Ishmael despite knowing Isaac would carry his covenant; Isaac loved Esau even as Jacob embodied his spiritual legacy. Fathers, it seems, struggle to see past birth order and recognize their true heir.

Once again, it fell to a determined woman to correct the course of history. Batsheva, Solomon's mother, understood what David did not yet perceive that. Solomon possessed unique gifts that would complete the work begun by King Saul and continued by David. Working with the prophet Nathan, she orchestrated a plan ensuring that the crown would pass to its rightful heir rather than simply its oldest claimant.

By the time Solomon ascended to the throne at age 12 in around 970 BCE, the kingdom had achieved something unprecedented in its prior history: genuine peace and prosperity. The security that Saul fought to establish and the spiritual vitality that David kindled created conditions that allowed Solomon to pursue an entirely different kind of monarchy. Where his predecessors were forced to focus on survival and internal development, Solomon could turn his attention outward, toward the broader world that surrounded his small but increasingly influential kingdom.

The Tanakh describes Solomon's reign in terms that seem almost utopian, as an era when Israelites "from Dan to Beersheba dwelt in safety, everyone under his own vine and under his own fig tree" (1 Kings 5:5). Solomon's kingdom represented the Golden Era of biblical history, when the knowledge of God could spread beyond Israel's small borders to reach all the nations of the world.

Despite King David's many extraordinary achievements, he carried one profound regret: his inability to build a permanent dwelling place for God in Jerusalem. The man who brought the Ark of the Covenant back to the holy city and established Jerusalem as Israel's eternal capital was forbidden from constructing the Temple that was his top priority and deepest dream.

As David explained to his son, God forbade him from building the Temple because he "shed much blood and fought great wars" (1 Chronicles 22:8). This divine decision revealed something crucial about the nature of the Temple. While warfare might be necessary to establish security and independence, it creates barriers to the spread of spirituality. Peace, by contrast, opens hearts and minds to wisdom and truth. David excelled at leading the nation victoriously in war, Solomon's very essence, his name and his generation, is one of peace:

> "David told his son Solomon: 'I had my heart set on building a temple for the name of the Lord, god. But this word of God came to me: 'You have shed much and fought great wars; you are not to build a house for My name, because you have shed much blood before Me. You will have a son who will be a **peaceful** man; I will give him

peace from all the enemies around him; his name will be **Solomon** (**peace** is his), and in his time I will give Israel **peace** and quiet." (1 Chronicles 22:7-9)

Whereas Saul was a warrior-king focused on physical survival and David a poet-warrior who combined military prowess with spiritual passion, Solomon embodied discerning wisdom that is the fruit of a mind at peace. The Torah testifies that "God gave Solomon wisdom and understanding beyond measure, and breadth of mind like the sand on the seashore" (1 Kings 5:9).

Solomon's approach to building the Temple reflected his universal vision. Rather than relying solely on Israelite resources, he reached out to neighboring kings, most notably Hiram, King of Tyre, who had maintained friendly relations with his father, King David.

"When Hiram heard the words of Solomon, he rejoiced greatly and said, 'Blessed be the Lord this day, who has given David a wise son over this great people'" (1 Kings 5:21). Hiram eagerly provided not only the finest cedar wood from Lebanon's forests but also master craftsmen skilled in stonework and metalworking. Hiram supplied building materials and the expertise that would transform the *Beit Hamikdash* into one of the wonders of the ancient world, built through an unprecedented partnership between Jewish wisdom and gentile craftsmanship.

Construction of Solomon's Temple began in the fourth year of his reign and required seven years to complete. But remarkably, though the building project was finished in the second month of the eleventh year, Solomon only dedicated the *Beit Hamikdash* in the first month of the twelfth year, on the holiday of *Sukkot* (Feast of Tabernacles). Why did King Solomon delay the dedication ceremony of the long awaited Temple for eleven months?

The answer has to do with the festival of Sukkot, the most universal of Israel's three pilgrimage festivals. While Passover celebrates Israel's liberation from Egypt and Shavuot commemorates the giving of the Torah at Sinai, Sukkot looks forward to a time when all nations will recognize the God of Israel. The prophet Zechariah described this very scenario, "All who survive of all those nations that came up against Jerusalem shall make a pilgrimage year by year to bow low to the King Lord of Hosts and to observe the festival of Sukkot" (Zechariah 14:16).

During Sukkot, seventy sacrificial offerings were made on behalf of the seventy nations of the world. The central holiday prayers focused on rainfall, a universal need shared by all peoples. By selecting this festival for the Temple's dedication, Solomon was announcing something revolutionary. His *Beit Hamikdash* would not be a typical ancient temple serving only one particular people, but a "house of prayer for all nations" (Isaiah 56:7).

Solomon's dedication prayer made his universal mission explicit. He prayed not only for the Jew who would come to worship, but specifically for gentiles and foreigners as well:

> "If the foreigner, who is not of Your people Israel, comes from a distant land for the sake of Your name - for they shall hear about Your great name and Your mighty hand ... when he comes to pray toward this house, hear in heaven Your dwelling place, and grant all that the foreigner asks of You; thus the peoples of the earth will know Your name and revere You..., and they will recognize that Your name is attached to this house that I have built." (1 Kings 8:41-43)

This universal approach was utterly unprecedented in the ancient world. Egyptian temples served Egyptians, Babylonian temples served Babylonians, but Solomon's Temple was designed from its very foundation to serve all the nations.

The very structure of the *Beit Hamikdash* indicated its outward message in several key features. One of the elements of the Temple that makes an immediate impression is its large dimensions. Solomon's Temple is double the length and breadth (60 cubits x 20 cubits) and triple the height (30 cubits) of its predecessor, the Tabernacle. The utensils were also multiplied. As opposed to a single menora, table and washbasin, Solomon's Temple contained ten menoras, ten tables for the showbread and ten washbasins. An explanation for the increase, at least in terms of the menoras, is that ten candelabras hold seventy lights, corresponding to the seventy nations of the world.

This outward expression is also expressed by the two golden cherubim adorning the chamber that houses the Ark of the Covenant. In the Tabernacle, the two cherubim faced each other, but in Solomon's Temple, "they faced the house [Temple]" (2 Chronicles 3:13). One explanation for the two different directions could be the difference in roles played by the Tabernacle and Solomon's Temple. The Tabernacle was internally directed, intended for service within the Jewish people in the isolated society of the wilderness. In contrast, the cherubim of the Temple were aimed to make an impression on a wider population, to spread the name of God beyond Israel and were therefore projected to the outside world.

One final architectural detail echoes this outward theme. When constructing windows, "He made narrow windows high up in the temple walls" (1 Kings 6:4). The technical jargon has been smoothed over in translation, but the Hebrew phrase is a bit more complicated indicating that the windows were both *Shekufim* (transparent) and *Atumim* (Sealed). The rabbinic explanation suggests something unique and profound. Unlike other buildings where windows were meant to allow light in, the Temple windows were narrow inside but wide on the outside in order to radiate light outwards to illuminate the world.

The *Beit Hamikdash* became the centerpiece of Solomon's strategy to fulfill Israel's mission as a "light unto the nations." But the building itself was only one element of a comprehensive approach that used every tool of statecraft including diplomacy, trade, marriage alliances, and cultural exchange, to spread knowledge of the One God of Israel throughout the world.

Ultimately, Solomon's wisdom became legendary far beyond Israel's borders. Rulers and dignitaries traveled from across the ancient world to consult with the king who could solve any problem, settle any dispute, and provide insight into the deepest questions of human existence. The most famous of these visitors was the Queen of Sheba, who journeyed from Ethiopia to test Solomon's renowned wisdom.

The Queen came as a skeptic but left as a believer, declaring:

> "It was a true report which I heard in my own land about your words and your wisdom. However, I did not believe the reports until I came and my eyes had seen it. And indeed, the half was not told to me. Your wisdom and prosperity exceed the fame of which I heard." (1 Kings 10:6-7)

More significantly, the Queen of Sheba's encounter with Solomon left a permanent mark on her nation's religious identity. Ethiopian tradition maintains that she converted to worship of the God of Israel and that she and Solomon had a son together who became the founder of Ethiopia's royal dynasty. To this day, the Ethiopian Orthodox Church traces its roots to this ancient connection with Jerusalem, and millions of Africans consider themselves spiritual descendants of Solomon's kingdom.

Solomon's court became a center of learning and wisdom that attracted seekers from across the civilized world. Near Eastern sources describe scholars, merchants, and nobles making pilgrimages to Jerusalem to experience firsthand the prosperity and justice of Solomon's kingdom and to learn about the religious and ethical principles that were behind it.

SOLOMON'S MATRIMONIAL DIPLOMACY

Solomon's universal approach extended beyond religious matters into every aspect of his reign. In the ancient world, royal marriages were the primary mechanism for creating international alliances, and Solomon's extensive matrimonial diplomacy connected Israel to kingdoms across the region.

"And King Solomon loved foreign women" (1 Kings 11:1) which according to Rabbi Yossi in the Jerusalem Talmud, was because "he sought to attract them with words of Torah and draw them close to the divine presence." Solomon's seven hundred wives and three hundred concubines were part of a deliberate foreign policy to spread Judaism throughout the region to other cultures and civilizations.

King Solomon's marriage to Pharaoh's daughter symbolized Israel's arrival as a major regional power. Egypt was the ancient world's superpower, and this alliance elevated tiny Israel to a status unimaginable just a few generations earlier. Through similar marriages and treaties, Solomon created a network of relationships that extended Israel's influence from Egypt to the Euphrates.

The wise king also revolutionized Israel's economy, transforming it from an agricultural society into a major commercial power. Solomon's merchant fleets sailed to distant Ophir, returning with gold, silver, ivory, and exotic animals. His trading posts dotted the major commercial routes around the known world. The wealth that flowed into Jerusalem from these enterprises funded not only the Temple's construction but also an unprecedented building program that included palaces, fortifications, and entire cities.

Solomon's tremendous wealth is best summarized in Ecclesiastes, which he wrote towards the end of his life according to Jewish tradition:

> "I multiplied my possessions. I built myself houses and I planted vineyards. I laid out gardens and groves, in which I planted every kind of fruit tree. I constructed pools of water, enough to irrigate a forest shooting up with trees. I bought male and female slaves, and I acquired stewards. I also acquired more cattle, both herds and flocks, than all who were before me in Jerusalem. I further amassed silver and gold and treasures of kings and provinces; and I got myself male and female singers, as well as the luxuries of commoners - coffers and coffers of them.

> Thus, I gained more wealth than anyone before me in Jerusalem. In addition, my wisdom remained with me: I withheld from my eyes nothing they asked for, and denied myself no enjoyment; rather, I got enjoyment out of all my wealth. And that was all I got out of my wealth. Then my thoughts turned to all the fortune my hands had built up, to the wealth I had acquired and won - and oh, it was all futile and pursuit of wind; there was no real value under the sun!" (Ecclesiastes 2:4-11)

Solomon understood that material prosperity was merely a means to a higher end. His goal was not wealth for its own sake but the creation of conditions that would allow Israel's spiritual message to reach the far corners of the earth. A prosperous, peaceful, and just society in Israel would serve as a living demonstration of what could be achieved when a nation organized itself around God's principles.

Yet for all his extraordinary achievements, Solomon's reign contained the seeds of its own destruction. The very universalism that made his kingdom a light to the nations also exposed it to influences that would ultimately prove corrupting.

The Torah specifically warned against the temptations that would face Israel's future kings. "He shall not multiply wives for himself, or else his heart will turn away; nor shall he greatly increase silver and gold for himself" (Deuteronomy 17:17). Like Saul, who relied on his own moral compass rather than listening to God's instructions regarding Amalek, Solomon began to believe that his wisdom exempted him from divine commandments. Surely, he reasoned, he was wise enough to marry foreign princesses without being influenced by their gods, wealthy enough to accumulate treasure without becoming attached to it, and powerful enough to maintain many horses without concern about returning to Egypt.

The biblical narrative traces Solomon's gradual spiritual decline. At first, he influenced his many wives, drawing them toward worshipping the God of Israel. But gradually, the dynamic reversed. "When Solomon was old, his wives turned his heart away after other gods; and his heart was not wholly devoted to the Lord his God, as the heart of David his father had been" (1 Kings 11:4). The king who prayed for foreigners to come and worship in Jerusalem began building shrines to regional gods to accommodate his wives' religious practices. The monarch who dedicated the Temple as a house of prayer for all nations began allowing idol worship in the very city where God's Temple stood.

Solomon's experience offers both inspiration and caution. His achievements demonstrate the extraordinary potential that emerges when Jewish wisdom and values are confidently shared with the broader world. The Temple, the diplomatic alliances, the cultural flowering, and the economic prosperity of Solomon's reign all testify to what becomes possible when Israel fulfills its role as a light unto the nations.

Nevertheless, Solomon's failures reveal the dangers that accompany a universal mission. The very openness that allows Jewish values to influence others also creates opportunities for external influences to corrupt Jewish identity and purpose. Universalism without boundaries becomes relativism, while mission without distinctiveness loses its power to transform. The key insight from Solomon's reign is that Israel can serve as a blessing to all nations only by remaining faithful to its own unique calling and identity. The moment Jews begin to compromise Judaism's essential elements in order to accommodate others, the universal mission collapses.

On the surface, King Saul appears to be the tragic leader while King Solomon represents the Golden Era. In reality, Saul's kingdom, however imperfect, allowed David to build upon it, adding a spiritual dimension that moved Israel closer to fulfilling its ultimate destiny. Solomon, on the other hand, whose mission was to influence the outside world, was instead corrupted by it, making him the truly tragic figure. Rather than assuming his messianic role as the Son of David who would spread the knowledge of God to the ends of the earth, Solomon became the last ruler of a unified Kingdom of Israel. Tragic indeed.

This failure left Israel's mandate to be a light unto the nations for future generations. The question is whether we will learn from Solomon's achievements and his errors. Can we avoid the pitfalls that destroyed him while embracing the universal vision that made his reign a golden age?

King Solomon's outward focus created another dangerous blind spot. His attention was fixed on the far horizons of diplomatic relations with distant monarchs, trade expeditions to exotic lands, and the construction of magnificent buildings that would showcase Israel's glory to the world. But while Solomon gazed outward, discontent was growing among those closest to home.

The king's ambitious building projects came at an enormous cost to his own people. The seven year building of the Temple and the thirteen year construction of the palace complex, along with fortified cities throughout the kingdom, required massive taxation and forced labor that grew increasingly burdensome for the masses. Their national pride in these monumental achievements gradually transformed into resentment among the common people who bore the weight of Solomon's grand vision.

Into this environment of growing dissatisfaction stepped Jeroboam, a talented and ambitious young man from the tribe of Ephraim. Solomon, recognizing his capabilities, appointed him to oversee the laborers working on the royal building projects. But Jeroboam's daily contact with the workers gave him intimate knowledge of their suffering, and his popularity grew as he became their advocate and voice.

The crisis came to a head when Solomon died and his son Rehoboam inherited the throne. Rehoboam possessed neither his father's wisdom nor his political instincts. When representatives approached him requesting relief from the crushing taxes and forced labor that had funded Solomon's building projects, the young king faced his first test.

Rehoboam's advisors were divided. The older counselors, who had served his father faithfully, urged him to show compassion and reduce the people's burden. "If you will be a servant to this people today and serve them, and answer them and speak good words to them," they advised, "then they will be your servants forever" (1 Kings 12:7). But Rehoboam's young companions, raised in the same privileged isolation as the new king, counseled harshness and a display of strength.

In a moment of tragic hubris, Rehoboam chose the path of arrogance over wisdom. Rather than offering relief, he added insult to injury and boasted that he would increase their burden. "My father made your yoke heavy," he declared to the laborers, "but I will add to your yoke; my father chastised you with whips, but I will chastise you with scorpions" (1 Kings 12:14).

This spectacular miscalculation ignited the simmering discontent that was building for years. The kingdom that Saul established, that David elevated and Solomon projected outward, was instantly torn apart. The ten northern tribes revolted and crowned Jeroboam as their king, forming what would become known as the Kingdom of Israel. Rehoboam was left ruling only his own tribe of Judah and Benjamin, the tribe that produced Israel's first king, Saul. This southern remnant became the Kingdom of Judah, governing from Jerusalem but controlling only a fraction of its original domain.

The division proved catastrophic for both kingdoms. What had once been a unified nation capable of influencing the known world became two rival states that spent their energies fighting each other. The northern kingdom, cut off from Jerusalem and the Temple, descended into idolatry as Jeroboam established alternative worship sites to prevent his subjects from making pilgrimages to Jerusalem. The southern kingdom, while maintaining the Temple service, lost most of its territory, population, and international influence. The rest of biblical history became a tragic tale of Israel's decline, rivalry, and missed opportunities. Internally weakened by division and spiritually compromised by foreign influences, they became vulnerable to the great empires that dominated the ancient world.

The end came in stages, each more devastating than the last. In 722 BCE, the mighty Assyrian Empire conquered the northern Kingdom of Israel, deporting its population and scattering the famous Ten Lost Tribes across their vast empire. The southern Kingdom of Judah survived another century and a half, but in 586 BCE, the Babylonian Empire destroyed Jerusalem, burned Solomon's magnificent Temple to the ground, and carried the surviving population into exile.

The psalmist captured the despair of a people who were once on top of the world: "By the rivers of Babylon, there we sat and wept when we remembered Zion" (Psalm 137:1). Yet even in the darkest hour, the prophet Jeremiah offered hope that their exile would soon end. "This whole land shall be a desolation and an astonishment, and these nations shall serve the king of Babylon seventy years" (Jeremiah 25:11). He promised that within a century God would restore His people to their land.

FROM NATION TO RELIGION

Jeremiah's prophecy proved remarkably accurate. The Babylonian Empire, which appeared to be all-powerful, was quickly conquered by the Persian Empire under Cyrus the Great. In 538 BCE, seventy years after the destruction of Jerusalem, Cyrus issued a decree allowing the Jewish exiles to return to their homeland and rebuild their Temple:

> "Thus says Cyrus king of Persia: All the kingdoms of the earth the Lord God of heaven has given me. And He has commanded me to build Him a house at Jerusalem, which is in Judah. Who is among you of all His people? May his God be with him, and let him go up to Jerusalem, which is in Judah, and build the house of the Lord God of Israel (He is God), which is in Jerusalem." (Ezra 1:2–3)

It was during this Babylonian exile that the Judeans from the former Kingdom of Judah became known as "Jews" for the first time. The exile scattered Jews throughout the region, creating diaspora communities that would become a permanent feature of Jewish life. The word "Jew" literally means "from Judea" - even as they spread across the world, the indigenous connection to the land remained embedded in the people's name.

Persecution also became a permanent feature of diaspora life. The Book of Esther, written during this period, tells how Esther and Mordechai saved Persia's Jews from genocide. The would-be exterminator was Haman, a descendant of Amalek - the ancient enemy King Saul had failed to destroy.

The return to Jerusalem marked the beginning of the Second Temple period. Under Persian sponsorship, returning exiles rebuilt the Temple, though it was but a shadow of Solomon's magnificent structure. Ezra and Nehemiah led efforts to restore Jewish religious and communal life, but the Jews who returned to their homeland found a very different world from the one their grandparents had left. They enjoyed none of the independence, prosperity, or international influence they had known during the First Temple period.

Instead, Judea would remain a small province within vast empires. First Persian, then Greek under Alexander the Great and his successors, and finally Roman. There was a brief period of independence under the Hasmonean dynasty, established by the Maccabees in the 2nd century BCE, but even this famous dynasty lasted only about eighty years before Roman power overwhelmed them. Under Roman rule, tensions escalated between Jewish hopes for independence and imperial demands for submission. After 420 years of semi independence, heavy taxation, and religious persecution, the Romans finally destroyed the Second Temple in 70 CE.

As devastating as the destruction of the Second Temple was, the Jewish people found within this catastrophe crucial lessons that would not only help them survive the centuries that followed, but would contain the seeds for the ultimate restoration of Israel in the future. In the decades leading up to the destruction, divisive sectarianism tore Israel apart. Rival factions such as the Pharisees, Sadducees, Essenes, and other sectarian groups, became bitter political enemies whose animosity toward one another invited danger from the outside.

The Jewish historian Josephus records that when the Roman general Vespasian came to attack Jerusalem, he observed the infighting taking place within the city walls and reportedly declared, "Let us sit as spectators while the Jews are torn to pieces by their civil wars." The Talmud reaches a sobering conclusion about the true cause of the downfall. In the end, it wasn't Rome that destroyed Jerusalem "It was on account of *sinat chinam* (baseless hatred) that the Temple was destroyed."

Once again, the Jews were kicked out of their land. This time, however, the exile would not last seventy years, but would continue for nearly two millennia.

As Jews scattered across the world, something fundamental changed about their national identity and mission. The nation of Israel, in any meaningful political sense, ceased to exist. What had once been a sovereign people capable of influencing regional affairs became a dispersed religious minority whose day to day goal was simply survival.

Where ancient Israel had been a nation among nations, with its own land, language, government, and culture, Judaism became defined primarily as a religion practiced by vulnerable minorities living at the sufferance of others. Christians saw the Jewish exile as divine punishment for rejecting Jesus, a theological interpretation that became a self-fulfilling prophecy as Christian societies systematically persecuted Jews living under their domain for centuries. Under Muslim rule, Jews lived as *dhimmis*, second-class subjects required to pay special taxes and submit to humiliating restrictions designed to emphasize their inferior status.

Yet, through all these centuries of religious persecution and powerlessness, the Jewish people never abandoned their national aspirations. In synagogues from Spain to Poland, from Yemen to

Morocco, Jews prayed for the restoration of their Temple, the return of their exiles, and the coming of the Messiah who would establish God's kingdom on earth.

More incredibly, despite unending oppression at the hands of virtually every empire and civilization, Jews rarely developed a spirit of revenge or resentment toward the nations of the world. Instead, they internalized the best elements of every culture they encountered, absorbed the wisdom and knowledge of their host societies, and maintained their age-old ambition of serving as a light unto the nations.

In 9th century Babylonia, a prayer first appeared in Jewish prayer books that beautifully captures this universal dream. The second paragraph of the Alenu, woven together from numerous passages throughout the Hebrew Bible, remains a beloved prayer recited daily by Jewish worshippers.

> "Therefore we put our hope in You, Lord our God, that we may soon see the glory of Your strength, to remove idols from the earth and cut off false gods (Isaiah 2:18; Ezekiel 30:13). Then the world will be perfected under the sovereignty of the Almighty (Zephaniah 3:9; Psalm 102:17), and all humanity will call upon Your name (Zephaniah 3:9; Isaiah 66:23), and the wicked of the earth will turn to You. All the inhabitants of the world will recognize and know that to You every knee must bow and every tongue swear loyalty (Isaiah 45:23).
>
> Before You, Lord our God, they will bow and fall, and give honor to Your glorious name (Isaiah 2:17; Psalm 72:11). They will all accept the yoke of Your kingship, and You will reign over them soon and forever. For the kingship is Yours, and You will reign in glory forever and ever, as it is written in Your Torah: 'The Lord shall reign forever and ever' (Exodus 15:18). And it is said: 'The Lord

shall be King over all the earth; on that day the Lord shall be One and His name One.' (Zechariah 14:9)"

This broad vision, embodied in prayers like *Alenu*, sustained Jewish communities through the darkest periods of their history. Even when they possessed no political power, controlled no territory, and commanded no armies, Jews always maintained their belief that their ultimate purpose was to help bring about the universal recognition of God that would transform the whole world.

The tragedy is that for nearly two thousand years, the Jewish people lacked the means to fulfill this mission. Scattered, powerless, and preoccupied with survival, they could do little more than preserve their traditions, maintain their communities, and hope that somehow, someday, God would restore them to their land and their higher purpose.

This hope seemed increasingly impossible as the centuries passed. Yet as the modern period dawned, forces were set in motion that would make the impossible inevitable. The same God that had sustained the Jewish people through their long exile was preparing to write the next chapter in their extraordinary story, and in humanity's journey toward its ultimate destiny.

THE DIGNITY OF DIFFERENCE

This remarkable Jewish commitment to universal redemption, sustained through two millennia of exile, has deep roots in the Torah itself.

While Judaism focuses on the particulars of one people, the Jewish God is universal. The Torah reflects this tension by beginning with the most universal story possible - the creation of the world and all of mankind - before narrowing its focus to one individual, Abraham, then one family, and finally one nation.

As British Chief Rabbi Jonathan Sacks (1948-2020) explained, "God, the creator of humanity, having made a covenant with all humanity, then turns to one people and commands it to be different in order to teach humanity the dignity of difference." Like a loving parent who gives each child a different path suited to their unique gifts, all nations have their own roles to play, but God gave Abraham's descendants a distinct role in the human story.

From the beginning, Jews were called to be different. Abraham was known as *Ha-Ivri* - "the Hebrew" - which literally means "from the other side of the river." The Torah repeatedly commands the Jewish people not to assimilate but to maintain their distinctiveness: "You shall not follow the customs of the land of Egypt where you dwelled, or of the land of Canaan where I am bringing you" (Leviticus 18:3). Later, God declares, "I have set you apart from other peoples to be Mine" (Leviticus 20:26).

Rabbi Sacks noted, "Judaism is a particularistic monotheism. It believes in one God but not in one religion, one culture, one truth. The God of Abraham is the God of all mankind, but the faith of Abraham is not the faith of all mankind." From its origins with Abraham, Judaism made way for a future that would maintain the dignity of difference.

God's covenant with Abraham contained two revolutionary elements. First, it connected a specific people to a specific land. "all the land that you see, to you I will give it, and to your seed forever" (Genesis 13:15). Second, it established that this particular people in this particular land would become the source of blessing for all humanity: "In you all the families of the earth shall be blessed" (Genesis 12:3).

The Hebrew word *nivrekhu*, "shall be blessed," comes from an agricultural term. *Mavrikh* describes how farmers bend branches toward the earth through layering. The branch stays connected to the source tree while taking root in new soil, creating a stronger, healthier plant. According to the medieval commentator Rashbam, Abraham's blessing works the same way. Other nations draw spiritual nourishment by staying connected to the Jewish people, who remain rooted in their covenant with God. The stronger that connection, the greater the blessing.

God loves all people, all nations, all religions. He made covenants not only with Israel but with all of Abraham's descendants - promising Ishmael he would become "a great nation" and assuring Esau of material blessings. Unlike religions that seek to convert others, Judaism respects the distinct paths God has given to different peoples. According to Jewish thought, righteous gentiles receive heavenly reward, and because they choose their spiritual path rather than inherit it through covenant, they achieve something even greater than Jews born into theirs.

Judaism only wants what is best for every man woman and child and gives many opportunities for non-Jews to achieve the highest levels of spiritual fulfillment. According to Jewish tradition, Moses translated the Torah into seventy languages before entering Israel to emphasize that every nation would have equal access to divine wisdom.

The Torah frequently refers to individual non-Jews who recognized God's hand on behalf of Israel. In the wilderness, Jethro (Exodus 18) heard about the miracles of the Exodus and came to serve as an advisor to Moses. Upon entering the land, Rahab (Joshua 2) helped Joshua's spies evade detection from the king of Jericho. During the period of the Judges, Ruth sacrificed her own future and chose to join the Jewish people. In the First Temple period, King Hiram (I Kings 5) assisted Solomon's Temple construction, and in the era of the Second Temple, Cyrus the Great (Ezra 1) enabled the return from Babylonian exile.

Yet these figures were the exception. As a whole, the nations surrounding Israel remained hostile. The prophets looked forward to a time when the recognition of Israel's destiny would no longer be limited to individuals, but would spread to entire peoples, heralding a new age of universal acknowledgment of God.

The prophet Zechariah wrote about this with breathtaking beauty:

> "And many peoples and mighty nations shall come to seek the Lord of Hosts in Jerusalem, and to entreat the favor of the Lord. Thus says the Lord of Hosts: In those days ten men from every language of the nations shall take hold, they shall take hold of the cloak of a Jew, saying: 'We will go with you, for we have heard that God is with you'" (Zechariah 8:22-23).

Today, with Israel restored to its homeland, we are witnessing a dramatic reversal of nearly two thousand years. No longer is support for the Jewish people limited to a handful of righteous individuals scattered across the nations. For the first time in history, millions of Christians openly stand with the State of Israel - not in spite of their faith, but because of it. This remarkable transformation marks the largest gentile movement in history to embrace the Jewish people and hold the key to unlocking God's blessings for the nations.

TURNING JUDAISM OUTWARDS

Despite the unprecedented support for Israel today, how can the Jewish people overcome centuries of justified fear and skepticism to embrace their universal mission that our generation requires? How can the State of Israel transition from inward facing Religious Zionism to outward facing Universal Zionism?

The answer comes from an unlikely source - a well known Hasidic rabbi whose movement was initially among Zionism's fiercest opponents, but who became one of Israel's most effective advocates.

We have seen how the Chabad Hasidic movement rejected Political Zionism from its inception, with the fifth Lubavitcher Rebbe warning that Zionists were "far more cunning in their evil" than secular assimilationists. Yet ironically, the model for Universal Zionism emerges from within this very movement through the revolutionary leadership of the seventh Lubavitcher Rebbe, Rabbi Menachem Mendel Schneerson (1902-1994).

Known simply as "the Rebbe," his brilliance and charisma transformed not only his own Hasidic community, but also reshaped Judaism's relationship with the wider world.Born in a village in Ukraine, educated at the Sorbonne in Paris, and ultimately establishing a dynasty in Crown Heights, Brooklyn, the Rebbe led a traumatized people in picking themselves up from the despair of the Holocaust and created a religious renaissance in the process.

In response to Hitler's obsession with eradicating every Jew, the rebbe developed an equally relentless passion to reach out to every Jew and draw them closer to God. Against all odds, he launched the most ambitious outreach campaign in Jewish history, even as he demanded from his followers the highest standards of Torah study and uncompromising religious observance. He sent young couples to the most distant corners of the world to serve as his emissaries and carry out his unique mission.

Under the Rebbe's leadership, Chabad established a global network of selfless followers who committed their entire lives to building Jewish communities in remote corners of the world. From Alaska to Thailand, from university campuses to isolated Jewish communities in places like Wyoming and Iceland, these rabbinic families bring Torah education, kosher food, and Jewish celebration to Jews who had never experienced their heritage. The Rebbe's directive to his disciples was to "Light up the world," which he fulfilled literally, through public menorahs during Chanukah, and spiritually, by spreading Torah wisdom.

Crown Heights became a pilgrimage destination to thousands of diverse Jews who lined up patiently outside the Rebbe's modest red brick home every Sunday to receive his blessing and a dollar bill to give to charity. His days were spent in prayer and study while throughout the night, the Rebbe would meet with visitors offering his sage advice. Rarely sleeping and never once taking a day off in many decades of service, he was driven by an inexhaustible commitment to the physical and spiritual welfare of each and every person he encountered.

The Rebbe's relationship with Zionism was complex, shaped by his need to honor his predecessors' philosophical opposition while responding to contemporary realities. A long line of previous Chabad leaders had firmly established an ideology that officially shunned the Zionist movement and so he rejected certain ceremonial aspects of political nationalism. For example, the Rebbe discouraged his emissaries from waving the Israeli flag at their Chabad Houses or singing the "Hatikvah" at their events, yet his practical and tangible love for the land and the people of Israel was unmatched.

In the tense weeks leading up to the Six-Day War, many American yeshiva students studying in Israel asked the Rebbe whether they should return home. His response was unequivocal: under no circumstances should they leave the Holy Land. Instead, he gave them a mission. The Rebbe taught that *Tefillin* (phylacteries) were the Jewish people's secret weapon in times of danger and instructed his followers to mobilize to spread their observance. The very next day, Chabad emissaries across Israel began approaching soldiers and civilians, urging them to don *Tefillin*, many for the first time in their lives.

The rest of the story is well known. Israeli jets launched their surprise attack, and in six extraordinary days, Israel defeated the combined armies of Egypt, Jordan, Syria, Iraq, and Lebanon - one of the greatest victories in military history. Following Israel's stunning win, Chabad established a permanent presence at Jerusalem's newly liberated Western Wall. To this day, visitors to the Kotel encounter Chabad volunteers offering to help them wrap *Tefillin*, continuing the Rebbe's legacy in providing spiritual security for his beloved Jewish people.

The Rebbe's concern extended beyond religious observance to Israel's military, political, and economic well-being. He followed Middle Eastern affairs with remarkable detail, and regularly hosted Israeli officials and politicians in Crown Heights for substantive policy discussions. When the issue of land for peace came up, he uncompromisingly opposed any territorial withdrawal. When Arab armies threatened, he consistently supported preemptive strikes against Israel's enemies. Like Rav Kook, the Rebbe viewed Israel's security not as a political question alone, but as a sacred responsibility bound up with the unfolding of divine redemption.

SEVEN UNIVERSAL LAWS OF NOAH

Remarkably, for a Hasidic leader who spoke primarily Yiddish and adhered to strictly traditional dress and customs, the Rebbe possessed a profound appreciation for all humanity. His deep love and concern for all of God's children moved him to launch a series of outward-facing campaigns through the expanding Chabad movement, directed especially toward non-Jews.

Appreciating the freedom that America provided, the Rebbe recognized that the United States was a unique and special country. In the 1960s, he boldly championed prayer in American public schools at a time when liberal Jews were at the forefront of the fight to remove religious expression from the school system and the public square. He firmly believed that acknowledging divine authority was essential for societal health and feared the consequences of American children abandoning the daily ritual.

Even more boldly, the Rebbe directed his emissaries to educate non-Jews about the Torah's Seven Universal Laws, also known as the Noahide commandments. Just as he urged his followers to stand on busy street corners inviting Jewish pedestrians to put on Tefillin or light Shabbat candles, he also launched campaigns encouraging non-Jews to observe the Seven Universal Laws.

The Rebbe taught that a single good deed by anyone - Jew or gentile - could have cosmic heavenly consequences and must be enthusiastically encouraged

According to Jewish belief, while Jews alone are bound by the Torah's 613 unique laws, all humanity shares seven fundamental moral obligations:

1. **Prohibition of idolatry** - Recognize one God
2. **Prohibition of blasphemy** - Respect God's name
3. **Prohibition of murder** - Preserve human life
4. **Prohibition of sexual immorality** - Maintain family sanctity
5. **Prohibition of theft** - Respect others' property
6. **Prohibition of eating flesh from a living animal** - Show mercy to animals
7. **Establishment of courts of justice** - Create fair legal systems

The Rebbe's campaign for the Seven Universal Laws provides a perfect template for interfaith cooperation in our generation. Instead of continuing to focus on theological differences that divide us, Jews and Christians can unite around the moral foundations that we share, recognizing that these universal principles derive from the same divine revelation at Sinai that both communities revere.

The Rebbe's extraordinary success in transforming Judaism from an inward-facing religion into a global outreach movement offers crucial lessons for our generation in transitioning towards Universal Zionism. He demonstrated that maintaining uncompromising dedication to Jewish tradition and Torah study need not conflict with passionate engagement with the broader world. Indeed, confidence in one's own identity is the foundation for meaningful relationships with others.

WE WANT MESSIAH NOW!

Of all the campaigns the Rebbe championed, none was more dramatic than his constant call for messianic redemption and the urgent cry that the time for the *Mashiach* (Messiah) was Now!" In the shadow of the Holocaust, he believed his generation stood closer than ever to the dawn of the messianic era. He urged Jews everywhere to study, pray, and actively prepare for this transformation, insisting that such efforts could hasten its arrival.

His followers put up billboards, ran newspaper advertisements, and distributed bumper stickers around the world proclaiming, "We Want Moshiach Now!" Many came to believe that the Rebbe himself was the awaited Messiah, a conviction that persisted even after his passing in 1994.

For many Jews, the Rebbe continues to embody their clearest vision of what the Messiah might be. Yet this raises a difficult question: can the Messiah be someone who has already died? This issue lies at the heart of one of the great theological disagreements between Judaism and Christianity.

Within Jewish tradition, there are defined criteria for the Messiah and a detailed portrait of the Messianic Age. The most systematic presentation of these ideas was given by Moses Maimonides (1135–1204), known as the Rambam, whose writings remain the foundation for Jewish thought on redemption.

Maimonides was born in Spain, but after fleeing Muslim persecution he eventually settled in Egypt. There he served as the royal physician for Sultan Suladin while simultaneously leading the local Jewish community near Cairo. On top of those responsibilities, Maimonides wrote monumental works of Jewish law and philosophy that are still studied daily by Torah scholars worldwide.

He concluded his massive legal code with a section called, "The Laws of Kings and Wars," describing what will happen when the Jews return to Israel, a return he saw as divinely promised and therefore requiring detailed explanation. Maimonides began this section with an important caveat:

> "All these and similar matters, one cannot know how they will happen until they happen. For these issues were hidden by the prophets. Even the sages did not have a clear tradition about these things, only their own interpretations. Therefore, there is no clear way to know them until they happen. The essential thing is not to dwell on the details of these matters, and one should not treat the *midrashim* (rabbinic writings) about them as absolute for they were never meant to be precise."

Despite this caveat, Maimonides provided practical criteria for identifying the Messiah. According to his framework, any person who is from the tribe of Judah and a descendant of King David, devoted to Torah study and observance, who successfully leads the Jewish people in following God's laws and fights to defend Israel, may be considered a potential Messiah. If this Messianic candidate then succeeds in rebuilding the Temple in Jerusalem and gathering the Jewish exiles back to their homeland, he is established with certainty as the Messiah son of David.

For Maimonides, the messianic age will not involve supernatural changes to the natural world. Instead, it would bring profound political and spiritual transformation. Most crucially, the Jewish people will no longer live under foreign oppression or be dependent on foreign nations financially or militarily, but be sovereign and secure in their homeland. The world will continue as is, but without war, persecution, or injustice. Freed from the brutal struggle for survival, humanity will devote itself fully to developing a relationship with the Almighty, pursuing wisdom, and perfecting the world.

As previously discussed, Rav Kook added a dimension by outlining not one but two messiahs. Messiah the son of Joseph will bring material restoration and the establishment of political sovereignty. This messiah will die before completing his work and only then will the Messiah son of David appear to complete the spiritual transformation. In Rav Kook's vision, Herzl's Political Zionism represents the Messiah son of Joseph, creating the framework for Jewish restoration but requiring future generations to complete the spiritual dimensions of redemption.

Returning to the question of whether the Rebbe could be the Messiah, much depends on how one defines the messianic role. Yet as Maimonides cautioned, "the essential thing is not to dwell on the details." Jewish history offers painful lessons about the dangers of becoming too fixated on messianic figures while forgetting the greater purpose: the political and spiritual transformation that draws all of humanity closer to God. Debate on the Messiah's identity is legitimate, but when it descends into conflict, it becomes destructive rather than redemptive.

If Jews and Christians are to take meaningful steps toward reconciliation, humility is essential. Christians, see Jesus as the Messiah which is a belief that should be respected by Jews. Indeed, Maimonides himself acknowledged a providential role in Christian messianic belief, recognizing that Jesus helped "prepare the way for the King Messiah" by spreading knowledge of the Bible across the world.

"But the thoughts of the Creator of the world are beyond human comprehension. For our ways are not His ways, nor our thoughts His thoughts. All these matters of Jesus of Nazareth and of that Ishmaelite who arose after him are only to prepare the way for the King Messiah, and to repair the whole world to serve God together, as it is said: 'For then will I turn to the peoples a pure language, that they may all call upon the Name of the Lord, to serve Him with one consent' (Zephaniah 3:9). Thus the whole world has already become full of the words of the Messiah, the words of the Bible, and the commandments. These have spread to the far islands and to many nations with uncircumcised hearts." (Laws of Kings and Wars, 11:4)

Accordingly, Jews can disagree with Christians on whether Jesus fulfilled the Messianic criteria, while simultaneously respecting Christians for their belief. This agreement to disagree has been famously captured in the joke that when the Messiah finally arrives in Jerusalem, Jews and Christians will both be standing together in Jerusalem. They will then nervously ask him, "Is this your first or second time here?" As long as it is not forced upon them, Christian belief in Jesus should not bother Jews, since, as Maimonides reminds us, "one cannot know how they will happen until they happen."

The crucial point is that both Jews and Christians await the same ultimate outcome. We are both eagerly awaiting the coming of the Messiah so that humanity can devote itself fully to knowing God, pursuing wisdom, and perfecting the world with peace and justice. And if we all truly want "Moshiach Now!" we must apply the pro-active lessons of Zionism to stop waiting passively and start taking action.

For much of modern history, Religious Zionism and Christian Zionism advanced along separate tracks - Jews building within the

Land of Israel while Christians supported from afar. Yet these efforts largely remained in silos, with few meaningful relationships between Jews and Christians. That era of parallel tracks must now give way to genuine partnership.

The messianic age can only come closer through the active cooperation of all who share the ancient hope of redemption. Universal Zionism offers our generation a unique opportunity to turn messianic longing into lived reality, by building faith-based relationships carefully, but also with urgency.

CHALLENGES OF RECONCILIATION

The spiritual revolution of our time has opened unprecedented possibilities for Jewish-Christian reconciliation, yet significant challenges remain. For too long, so-called "interfaith dialogue" often served as little more than a cover for persecution - especially when the conversation turned to our shared Holy Scriptures.

In the medieval era, Christians often dragged Jews into forced public debates, using the Bible itself as a weapon against Jewish faith. Even the great sage Nachmanides, after brilliantly defending Judaism before the King of Aragon in 1263, was nevertheless accused of blasphemy and driven into exile. Centuries later, Napoleon Bonaparte likewise compelled Jewish leaders to answer probing questions about the Torah in order to secure civil rights. In 1807 he convened a body of rabbis - dubbed "Napoleon's Sanhedrin" - with the clear aim of subordinating Jewish law to French authority.

These episodes reveal a recurring tragedy: the Torah, given for the benefit of all humanity, was repeatedly turned against the Jewish people. Small wonder that Jews have often been wary of discussing Torah with non-Jews. Yet for reconciliation to be genuine, such conversations must take place - focused not on polemics, but on shared values and the transmission of Torah's wisdom to the world.

Thankfully, today's reality is fundamentally different. The Jewish people are no longer powerless subjects of foreign rulers but sovereign in their own land, where Jewish identity and Torah study thrive as never before. Moreover, many Christians now approach Jews not to assert superiority, but to learn. Christian Zionist leaders openly credit the Jewish people with their greatest treasure - the Bible itself. No longer persecuted on account of the Torah, Jews now encounter sincere Christians who approach the Jewish People with profound gratitude.

Rabbi Kook wrote about this reconciliatory milestone in the grand process of redemption:

> "When the time comes for the light of the world to be revealed, it will become known to humanity that we have shared the path of life, of true pleasure, without which life is lacking all meaning. Every man can appreciate pleasure and happiness, and they will come to honor and treasure the people who are its source." (Orot Yisrael 5:15)

The Christian embrace of Jewish restoration creates a unique historical moment. As hundreds of millions of Christians worldwide have recognized God's hand in Israel's rebirth, the Jewish people themselves are experiencing their unique profound spiritual awakening and rediscovering their own relationship with God. The catalyst for this Jewish revival has been the crucible of war itself.

Universal Zionism insists that this religious revival pulsating through Israel since October 7th, is not meant to remain confined to the Jewish people. Especially now, such outward focus could provide tremendous healing and purpose for Israelis grappling with war trauma while uniting different streams of

Israeli society around a shared mission larger than political divisions.

Much has been said here about Jewish-Christian reconciliation, but it's important to emphasize that this is only where Universal Zionism begins, not where it ends. The Universal God of Abraham is the God of all humanity, and the messianic era will ultimately embrace every nation and people. The reconciliation between Jews and Christians is the crucial first step in a process that will ultimately extend more broadly - first throughout Christianity, and then to Islam, a faith which, despite significant theological differences, does respect the Bible.

The Abraham Accords is the natural platform for building interfaith relations with moderate Muslims and expanding it will bring great blessings. Once this shared monotheistic foundation is strengthened, it can serve as a bridge to engage other nations and cultures across the globe.

Jews and Christians, however, share a uniquely strong foundation for unity. We are the only two major faiths that share the same Holy Scripture. Christianity emerged from and is built upon Judaism, making reconciliation not just possible but inevitable. This cooperation will naturally begin with those Christians who have already rejected Replacement Theology - the poisonous doctrine that claims God abandoned the Jews.

In recent decades, the rejection of Replacement Theology has spread outward from the United States. Across the world - from Nigeria to Fiji - Christians are renouncing this theological error. If this trend continues, humanity may soon witness something unprecedented: the two oldest monotheistic faiths no longer standing in opposition, but moving toward mutual recognition and partnership.

We cannot fathom the damage done when mankind tries to obstruct God's purposes, nor can we begin to imagine the blessings released when we become facilitators of the divine plan. The success that follows will be unlike anything experienced in human history, transforming lives on the individual, national, and global scale. When the world at last recognizes Israel as the land given by God to His chosen people, humanity will stand on the threshold of its ultimate destiny.

BUILDING THE UNIVERSAL ZIONIST MOVEMENT

The vision outlined here is not a definitive blueprint but an opening to a larger conversation about Israel's future role in the world. Having traced the journey from Political Zionism, through Religious Zionism, to the threshold of Universal Zionism, we now face the challenge of translating this historical progression into contemporary reality.

What follows is an initial attempt to imagine how Universal Zionism might take shape as a movement capable of reshaping the relationship between Israel and the nations. It draws on my experiences and conversations with hundreds of Jewish and Christian Zionists, but makes no claim to perfection.

The early Zionist movement thrived precisely because it embraced diverse voices, fierce debates, and constant refinement. Theodor Herzl's original vision was reshaped again and again as ideals met realities. Universal Zionism, too, must undergo this same process of adaptation and improvement.

In less than a century, the Jewish people have achieved what was once unthinkable: the return of the majority of world Jewry to its homeland, Israel's rise as an economic and military power, and the growth of Christian support from a few isolated figures to hundreds of millions of believers worldwide.

This convergence of circumstances creates a historic opportunity: the birth of a spiritual-political movement unlike anything humanity has seen, one that could bring renewal not only to Israel but to the world. Such a movement cannot emerge by chance or good will alone. It requires the same strategic vision, organizational structures, and disciplined planning that powered the first wave of Zionism.

Like Political Zionism before it, Universal Zionism must rest on three essential pillars: a core set of beliefs that provide ideological clarity, a political agenda that turns vision into action, and spiritual and cultural resources that can sustain it through inevitable challenges.

Its success will depend on broad participation. Whether Jewish or Christian, religious or secular, left or right, the call is the same: to engage seriously with this vision and contribute to its growth. History is waiting for those who will turn ancient promises into present realities, transforming the hope of millennia into the achievement of our generation.

What follows is one possible framework. The invitation is open for you to join in shaping the phase of the Zionist movement.

FOUNDATIONAL BELIEFS AND CORE PRINCIPLES

Before delving into practical steps, we must first identify the foundational beliefs shared by all Universal Zionists.

At the heart of Universal Zionism lies a simple but radical proposition: the Bible still means what it says about the Land of Israel. Jews and Christians who take Scripture seriously must support complete Jewish sovereignty over the territories God promised to the descendants of Abraham, Isaac, and Jacob. Sovereignty over the biblical heartland of Judea and Samaria is the most relevant and controversial issue surrounding Israel today and is the foundational belief that distinguishes Universal Zionism from mere political support for Israel.

The Torah's promise is neither ambiguous nor conditional. When God told Abraham, "All the land that you see, to you will I give it, and to your seed forever" (Genesis 13:15), He established an eternal covenant that no government or international organization possesses the authority to revoke.

For Jews and Christians who honor the Hebrew Bible as the Word of God, recognizing a Palestinian State in the land God gave to the descendants of Isaac exclusively is a hypocritical contradiction. If the Bible is true concerning issues such as salvation and eternal life, it must also be trustworthy concerning the boundaries of the Promised Land including Judea and Samaria.

The fulfillment of these promises is both an opportunity and an obligation for bible believers who profess belief in God's Word. One cannot celebrate God's faithfulness while supporting policies that demand Israel relinquish parts of its covenantal inheritance.

POLITICAL AGENDA: FROM BELIEF TO ACTION

Transforming religious conviction into political reality requires a nuanced strategy of international outreach, public diplomacy, and policy advocacy that learns from both the successes and failures of previous efforts on behalf of the State of Israel. The movement must simultaneously build grassroots support among faith based communities while engaging with political leadership at every level of government.

International outreach begins on a local level by transforming churches and synagogues into active centers for Israel education and advocacy training. Moving beyond superficial pro-Israel events, participating congregations would offer engaging classes covering Jewish history, Hebrew language, Israeli politics, and effective advocacy skills. These programs would attract the most committed members of the Jewish and Christian communities, creating opportunities for networking, relationship building and grassroot organizing.

Participants would discover that engagement with Israel brings a myriad of benefits to their own communities. Congregations affiliated with Universal Zionism would attract new members, while their advocacy training programs would develop leadership skills applicable to other community challenges.

Public diplomacy requires reframing the narrative around Israel from defensive arguments about security needs to positive assertions about moral and spiritual imperatives. Current consensus often begins by accepting the premise that Israeli control over Judea & Samaria illegitimate, then attempts to apologetically provide security-based rationales that sound increasingly unconvincing. Universal Zionism reverses this dynamic by confidently asserting that Jewish sovereignty over all of Israel represents the restoration of justice after centuries of colonial occupation by various empires. Rather than apologizing for Jewish presence in Hebron or Shiloh, Universal Zionists would celebrate the return of these cities' indigenous population after centuries of exile. Instead of defensive explanations about the legality of settlements, Universal Zionists would offer positive accounts of agricultural innovations that have transformed barren hilltops into thriving communities.

In an age rife with conspiracy theories targeting Jews and Israel, this reframing becomes especially powerful when delivered by non-Jews who cannot be easily dismissed or accused of dual loyalty. When pastors from rural states where there are very few Jews explain to their elected officials that supporting Israeli sovereignty represents their own faith, they transform a complex geopolitical calculation into a matter of local concern.

To support this diplomatic overhaul, Israel must expand its reach beyond the large Jewish population centers and establish a presence in cities with significant Christian Zionist populations.

These hubs would serve multiple functions, operating as business incubators that facilitate trade partnerships between Israeli companies and local businesses, and tourism centers that promote educational and pilgrim travel.

Cities that embrace partnerships with Israel would find themselves positioned to become high-tech, prosperous, and secure regional models as Israeli investment, expertise, and security cooperation help them address their own challenges. The same innovative approaches that have made Israel a global leader in cybersecurity, water management, and agricultural technology could revitalize struggling American cities while strengthening the bilateral relationship.

Policy advocacy must focus on lobbying for new legislation that strengthens Israel and the special US-Israel relationship. In today's post-October 7th reality, that begins with an effort to wean Israel off American foreign aid. Even though US aid to Israel has been critical and is mutually beneficial, Israel must become fully independent as an ally and partner of America, not a protectorate.

Israeli governmental policies can be explored to benefit faith based allies of Israel around the world. Right now, Israel's most committed Christian supporters are only eligible for 90 day tourist visas, which is a source of frustration to those who want to spend more time studying or volunteering. Innovative programs should offer non-prostelyzing Christian Zionists to obtain residency visas to live in strategic areas of Israel where their presence would contribute to demographic balance and economic development.

Many passionately pro-Israel Christians around the world face severe religious persecution from Muslims in their home countries. Just as Israel serves as a refuge for Jews, it could and should find ways to protect Christians facing violence at home while demonstrating a real commitment to defending religious liberty worldwide.

Just as many countries offer "Golden Passports" to high-net-worth individuals, Israel could develop a Virtual Israeli Citizenship enabling supporters worldwide to carry an Israeli passport - not as full citizens with voting rights, but as recognized allies with meaningful legal benefits. Such a program would create a formal bond between Israel and millions of supporters abroad. Governments inclined to pressure Israel because of their domestic Muslim populations would hesitate if large numbers of their own citizens held an official, legally recognized connection to the Jewish state.

This idea would naturally raise legitimate concerns within Israel's Jewish population. However, committees could be tasked with addressing these concerns while ensuring that the program strengthens Israel's security, economy, and diplomatic standing.

SPIRITUAL, SOCIAL, AND CULTURAL DIMENSIONS

The foundation of any lasting movement lies not in short term political calculations but in the deeper spiritual, social, and cultural bonds that sustain its members through inevitable setbacks and opposition. Universal Zionism must create institutions and experiences that transform casual supporters of Israel into committed participants whose lives are greatly enriched by their involvement.

Education is the most crucial area of investment for long-term movement building. Rather than the superficial "Israel 101" courses that currently characterizes most pro-Israel programming, Universal Zionism requires comprehensive curricula that teach both Jews and Christians that a fully sovereign Israel is a central rather than peripheral aspect of their faith.

According to a 2020 Pew study, while three-quarters of American Jews say that being Jewish is important to them, there is no single, uniform answer to what that means. Most Jewish adults identify remembering the Holocaust and working for justice and equality as "essential" to their Jewish identity. Interestingly, 34% consider having a good sense of humor essential, while only 41% say the same about supporting Israel. Universal Zionism must therefore provide relevant and engaging educational opportunities that help Jews rediscover and strengthen their connection to their homeland.

For Christian participants, education would focus on how the restoration of the Jewish people fits within their own faith. Programs would include in-depth Bible study taught by Christian theologians highlighting the Hebrew roots of Jesus and the New Testament, newly uncovered archaeological discoveries that confirm biblical history, and prophetic passages describing the vital role of the nations in supporting Israel's restoration.

Equally important, Christians must devote greater time and energy to studying the Hebrew Bible. Here, Jews can play a crucial role - guiding Christians through the original Hebrew and revealing the profound depth and layers of meaning within the Scriptures. Such study not only enriches Christian faith but also strengthens the bond between Jews and Christians as they discover, together, the living word of God.

Education is critically necessary at the college level. With so many overpriced universities becoming hotbeds for antisemitism and far left ideologies, parents and students are desperately seeking new models. Universal Zionism could step into the breach by providing world-class, Ivy League level courses both online and through campuses built throughout Israel servicing Jewish and non-Jewish international students. The long-term benefits to the State of Israel would be incalculable. Students would receive a top notch education at a very low cost, while developing a life long attachment to Israel and the Jewish people.

Tourism may be the most transformative tool for fostering lasting commitment to Universal Zionism. Despite its unparalleled historical and spiritual significance, Israel attracts far fewer visitors than countries with much less historical weight. France and Spain each welcome around 90 million tourists annually, while Israel's record year brought in just five million. Part of the problem lies in Israel's tourism marketing, which has often emphasized the wrong messages and destinations - resulting in Christians choosing to vacation elsewhere rather than engaging with the living history of the Holy Land.

Universal Zionism would revolutionize Israeli tourism by positioning the country as the premier destination for Christian education and spiritual development. Rather than brief visits, Christian pilgrims would be encouraged to spend extended periods studying Hebrew, exploring archaeological sites, and most importantly, building relationships with Jewish families through home hospitality and Shabbat experiences.

This tourism expansion would require massive infrastructure investment in highways, light rail systems, hotels, and educational facilities, creating an economic boom that would benefit both Israeli citizens and international visitors. Christians who return home after months of study in Israel would become natural ambassadors whose personal testimonies carry far more credibility than any professional advocacy campaign.

Charitable giving to Israel must radically evolve by recognizing 21st century realities. Throughout the 20th century, Jews gave generously and helped transform Israel from a poor country to a prosperous one. Today, Jewish communities in the diaspora are strapped with high costs of maintaining their own educational, religious and security infrastructure.

Universal Zionism must lead to a new and creative charitable partnership model built for our generation based on mutual benefit and shared destiny. Rather than one-way charitable donations that flow from the diaspora to Israel, Universal

Zionism must reverse that and focus more on building up pro-Israel communities around the world.

Just as Jewish communities have always taken care of their own members, Universal Zionism would create support networks that look after all those who love Israel, not just Jews. Universal Zionism could create caring communities of Zionists around the world who look out for one another and use their resources to build local institutions centered around Israel and fund trips for their young people to visit and study there.

Honoring Shabbat has long preserved the Jewish People as noted by Ahad Ha'am, "More than the Jews kept the Sabbath, the Sabbath has kept the Jews." It's time for a Shabbat Revolution where both Jews and Christians come together to grab their corner of the four-pillared civilizational tent that Charlie spoke about the day before he was killed.

After centuries of opposition, Jews and Christians have begun coming together, and we must accelerate that reconciliation. Universal Zionism calls for us to stop operating in separate silos and form a real alliance based on our shared values and common threats. This requires stepping out of our comfort zones and coming together over our love for Israel and appreciation for biblical traditions such as Shabbat. If this sounds trivial, it most surely is not. Perhaps the most influential relationship between a Christian and a Jew in our time has been forged over a shared love for the Torah and the Sabbath.

In an interview, Charlie Kirk explained that he first heard about Shabbat from Dennis Prager. Charlie claimed to have listened to more of Dennis Prager's Torah teachings than anyone else alive, "He would always talk about the Shabbat and I found myself, after a couple of years of hearing this, getting really jealous of him, being like, 'Wait a second! You're just able to unplug for one day and not work and be with friends and family and worship God? I want that!"

Charlie ended his popular podcast every Friday by wishing his listeners "Shabbat Shalom" and encouraging them to unplug by putting their cellphones in a drawer for 24 hours, like he did. "The Sabbath saved my life and helped preserve my family and my career," Kirk admitted.

With the publication of Charlie's book about Shabbat, there has never been more interest in the Jewish Sabbath. Christians are eager to experience an authentic Shabbat for themselves, and Jews should invite Christians into their homes on Friday night to share the magic with them.

The purpose of the blueprint outlined here is to stimulate ideas and conversations around Universal Zionism. It represents an ambitious vision that builds upon existing foundations while dramatically expanding their scope and effectiveness. Implementation would require further discussions and careful coordination between Israeli institutions, diaspora Jewish organizations, and Christian Zionist leadership to ensure that all participants are getting the most from their involvement while advancing the common goal of Universal Zionism.

Now comes the work of developing the leadership, and implementing the strategies that can transform this potential into reality. Even partially fulfilling some of these initiatives will allow Israel to begin fulfilling its destiny as a light unto the nations and blessing all the families of the earth.

A FINAL CALL TO ACTION

What was Hamas thinking?

On October 7, 2023, the terror group launched a barbaric assault on the most advanced military in the region - perhaps in the world. They knew they couldn't win a conventional war. And indeed, the outcome was catastrophic for Gaza: tens of thousands killed, Hamas leadership decimated, and the territory left in ruins. Did they not foresee this devastation?

Now that a ceasefire has been accepted, Hamas has declared victory. And, by their own twisted logic, they're not entirely wrong.

They didn't aim to defeat Israel militarily, they set out to win ideologically. In that realm, they've proven disturbingly effective. Israel's enemies operate tirelessly, and are far ahead in the propaganda war. They've mastered the art of narrative manipulation - turning lies into truth and truth into lies. They brand Israel a genocidal apartheid regime and call Jews occupiers, despite Israel being the only nation on earth to exist in the same land, speak the same language, and practice the same faith as it did thousands of years ago.

Hamas planned their psychological warfare meticulously: filming their atrocities with GoPros cameras, staging grotesque hostage spectacles, sparking campus uprisings, organizing flotillas, and coordinating diplomatic moves like European recognition of Palestinian statehood.

Israel, initially blindsided while fighting on seven military fronts, struggled to counter this propaganda blitz. But over time, it became painfully clear: to Hamas, the real battlefield is in the global court of opinion.

In *The Art of War*, Sun Tzu taught, "If you know the enemy and know yourself, you need not fear a hundred battles. If you are ignorant of the enemy but know yourself, your chances of winning or losing are equal. And if you are ignorant both of your enemy and of yourself, you will certainly succumb in every battle."

To win the information war, the battle over truth, we must recognize who our enemies are, who we are, and who our allies are. Many of Israel's long-standing allies, on both sides of the political aisle, have turned against the Jewish state, perhaps irreversibly. The left has completely embraced the Palestinian cause, while much of the right is falling prey to old antisemitic canards. This is jarring, disappointing, and unsettling. But while God has closed doors that once stood open, He is simultaneously opening doors that were closed for centuries. The very crisis over truth that has exposed the weakness of political alliances has revealed the strength of something far more powerful: faith-based partnerships rooted in biblical truth.

The Jewish-Christian alliance represents the very best path to victory in the battle for hearts and minds. When hundreds of millions of Christians around the world declare that their faith *requires* them to stand with Israel - when they understand that the promises made to Abraham are eternal and unbreakable, when they see attacks on the Jewish state as attacks on the God they worship - this creates a firewall that social media propaganda cannot penetrate. Unlike political coalitions that shift flimsily with electoral winds, ties between Jews and Christians that are based on our shared biblical values transcend temporal concerns and are rock solid.

Throughout this book, we have traced the remarkable progression from Political Zionism through Religious Zionism to Universal Zionism. Political Zionism gave us the body, and Theodor Herzl and David Ben-Gurion achieved the impossible by creating a sovereign Jewish homeland after two millennia of exile. But a body without a soul is merely a corpse, no matter how efficiently it functions.

Religious Zionism gave us the spirit - a return to spiritual purpose, a recognition that Jewish sovereignty means nothing if divorced from Jewish identity and divine mission. Rav Kook infused the Zionist project with meaning that transcended survival, connecting the return to the land with the ultimate redemption promised by the prophets. But a soul focused only inward fails to fulfill its purpose in the world.

Universal Zionism provides Israel with its contemporary mission to finally become the light unto the nations that was always its destiny. The body that Political Zionism built and the soul that Religious Zionism kindled must now turn outward to bless all the families of the earth.

Imagine a world where Jihadi attacks on Israel are immediately recognized by hundreds of millions of Christians as attacks on their own faith. Where campus activists who target Jewish students face organized opposition not just from Jewish organizations but from Christian groups across every denomination.

Imagine churches and synagogues in every city becoming centers for Israel education, where Jews and Christians forge friendships, study Torah and honor Shabbat together. Imagine thousands of Christian students spending summers in Israel, learning Hebrew, exploring archaeological sites, and building relationships with Israelis that will last a lifetime.

Imagine Israeli cities transformed by the influx of Christian supporters who invest their talents and their resources into strengthening the Jewish state. Imagine new institutions - universities, research centers, cultural exchanges - that become models for how different faiths can collaborate while maintaining their distinct identities. Imagine Israel becoming known not just for its military prowess or technological innovation but for pioneering a new model of interfaith cooperation that offers hope to a war-torn region and a divided world.

Unlike Herzl's *Altneuland*, this is not utopian fantasy. Every element described here is already happening on a small scale. Universal Zionism simply calls for expanding and accelerating what God has already begun and moving these relationships from the margins to the mainstream.

We have seen throughout this book how the Bible describes Solomon's reign as a golden age - a time when Israel's wisdom attracted foreign rulers from distant lands, when the Temple became a house of prayer for all nations, when peace and prosperity allowed the knowledge of God to spread throughout the world. Yet that golden age was incomplete and temporary. Solomon's compromises led to division, the Temple was destroyed, and the people were scattered.

The prophets Micah and Zechariah both use the idyllic language describing King Solomon's golden age to envision a future time when "everyone will sit under their own vine and fig tree" (Micah 4:4, Zechariah 3:10). The golden age we can build can even surpass Solomon's because it would avoid previous mistakes, rest on firmer foundations and embrace a broader vision.

With Israel's stunning military victories over its enemies, that promised era is within our grasp. We stand at the threshold of something unprecedented in human history - a time when millions of non-Jews are voluntarily aligning themselves with the God of Israel, and actively facilitating Jewish restoration rather than obstruct it.

Today is when the ancient promise that "all the families of the earth shall be blessed" through Abraham's descendants can become the modern reality. This is what Isaiah foresaw when they described nations streaming to Jerusalem to learn the Torah

(Isaiah 2). This is what the prophets meant when they wrote that gentiles would carry Jewish children on their shoulders back to their homeland (Isaiah 49) and help rebuild its ancient ruins (Isaiah 61). This is the fulfillment of *Hatikva* (the hope) that has sustained the Jewish people through two millennia of exile - the hope for the restoration of Israel and the entire world through their return.

Perhaps you're reading these words and thinking: this vision is inspiring, but what does it have to do with my life? I'm not a political or spiritual leader. The history of the Zionist movement demonstrates that we are all active participants in the unfolding of God's plan for history with the power to shape its direction.

We have seen how even a small number of ordinary individuals can alter the course of human events through the transformative power of a single idea. As Herzl observed, "No man is strong or wealthy enough to move a people; only an idea can do that." Today, we need a new generation of Universal Zionists to respond to the idea and complete the unfinished work of restoring both Israel and the world.

JOIN THE MOVEMENT

If you are Jewish or Christian and want to take action in this important stage of God's unfolding plan for history, the best way to get involved is to participate in the conversation.

Israel365 is leading the movement for a Jewish-Christian alliance on behalf of Israel and the nations, and are eager for more like-minded people to join us.

The best way to learn more is by scanning the QR code below or by visiting: **www.Universal-Zionism.com**

There you will find:

- Educational resources for deepening your understanding of Israel and the unique times we are in
- Opportunities to connect with like-minded Jews and Christians in your area over Shabbat and other events
- Information about trips to Israel that go beyond traditional tourism to build lasting relationships
- Updates on the growing Universal Zionist movement and how you can contribute

Israel365 Action is now officially bringing this vision of a new generation of pro-Israel supporters to the World Zionist Congress, the official Zionist movement established by Theodor Herzl himself. We are not merely another advocacy organization or charitable initiative, Universal Zionism is a movement that honors the past while embracing the future, by discovering profound unity in shared values. We are energized by this historical moment when Jews and Christians finally overcome centuries of division to fulfill our common destiny.

This is our generation's defining moment. We have been awakened by the horrors of October 7th and the alarming global response that followed on October 8th. Israel and Jews everywhere are facing unprecedented hatred based on falsehoods and hostility built on lies and the only way to fight back is with the truth. We are blessed today to live at a time when we are witnessing with our own eyes so much of the Bible coming true. God's promises for Israel and the world are eternal, unbreakable, and absolutely true.

The door that is opening leads to the greatest era in history because it fulfills divine promises and our deepest hopes. Instead of continuing to block God's blessings by preventing His mission for the world, every one of us can become active facilitators of His plan for Israel and the nations.

That era will be realized when Jews and Christians together honor what He honors and love what He loves. Together, we will ascend His sacred mountain as once promised:

> "As for the Nations who attach themselves to the Lord. To serve Him, and to love the name of the Lord, to be His attendants. All who observe the Sabbath and do not desecrate it. And who hold fast to My covenant, I will bring them to My sacred mountain And let them rejoice in My house of prayer. Their burnt offerings and sacrifices shall be welcome on My altar; For My House shall be called a house of prayer for all peoples."

(Isaiah 56:6-7)

Scan to join the Universal Zionist movement

ACKNOWLEDGMENTS

Whenever I meet someone new and they ask about Israel365, my standard elevator pitch is: "We are a Jewish organization that builds meaningful relationships with Evangelical Christians in order to strengthen Israel." I can quickly explain *what* we do, but it takes me a bit longer to explain *why*. I needed a simple way to articulate the deeper purpose and overarching vision behind our work.

Over the years, countless books have shaped my thinking and influenced Israel365's approach. To keep this book accessible, I've avoided footnotes, but the works and authors that impacted me most appear in the bibliography. I encourage interested readers to explore these sources.

The breakthrough in articulating our vision came from an unexpected but welcome source. My colleague at Israel365, Rabbi Elie Mischel introduced me to the writings of a scholar in Jerusalem named Pinchas Polonsky. He was born in Moscow in 1958 into a Jewish but atheist family who grew up knowing nothing about his heritage. Living under an oppressive Soviet regime where Judaism was severely restricted, Dr. Polonsky began to rebel against the regime by gathering with other Jews, studying Torah, and learning to pray in Hebrew. Brilliant and determined, Pinchas mastered even the most difficult works, including Rabbi Abraham Kook's philosophy, and translated much of it from Hebrew into Russian.

When I got to know Pinchas, I was immediately struck by his fresh and creative outlook shaped by his dramatic journey of discovering Judaism and Israel as an adult behind the Iron Curtain. Pinchas shared with Elie and me a thin booklet that he wrote called, *Universal Religious Zionism*. The title alone captivated me, and the bold ideas within delivered on its promise. Polonsky had developed a compelling model for our generation based on the ancient kings Saul, David, and Solomon, drawing a parallel between these three kings and modern Zionism's progression from political to religious to universal. His model gave me exactly what I needed: a simple yet profound way to articulate Israel365's larger vision.

I wanted to introduce Polonsky's ideas to a wider audience, but some of his material was a bit too complex for readers unfamiliar with Jewish sources and history. So I set out to expand and adapt his work for both Jews and non-Jews, to make these concepts accessible without sacrificing their depth. I'd like to sincerely thank Pinchas not only for sharing his groundbreaking ideas but for being so gracious in allowing me wide latitude to adapt his work here. He and his close associate, Alex Shylankivich, have no personal agenda - they simply want these universal ideas to reach as many people as possible. Israel365 is proud to republish Dr. Polonsky's other writings, such as *Universal Torah*, and I hope our partnership continues to expand his audience.

Pinchas introduced me to Dr. Dmitry Radyshevsky, a Harvard-educated theologian from a similar Russian background. Dmitry had wrestled with Judaism's relationship with Christianity and published his perspectives in 2006 under the title *Universal Zionism*. I didn't discover his book until after completing my manuscript. I'm grateful to Dmitry for graciously allowing me to use the same title - a fitting choice, since we share a common vision even as we approach it differently.

The ideas in this book were developed and refined through countless conversations with extraordinary colleagues that I get to work with every day at Israel365. I am especially grateful to Rabbi Elie Mischel and Rabbi Pesach Wolicki, whose deep thinking about the principles underlining Universal Zionism and how Israel can more effectively serve as a Light unto the Nations have been invaluable. Their insights helped sharpen my understanding and push these concepts forward.

This publication would not have been possible without the leadership of our CEO, Robbie Frohlinger, who urged me to write about Universal Zionism in the first place. Special thanks also go to our talented designer Yehudit Weingarten for the beautiful book cover; to Aharon Mendlowitz for the layout and typesetting; to Shira Schechter for her careful editing; and to Rafi Weinstein for managing production.

As Israel365 has grown our library - publishing a dozen books in just the past year - Rabbi Rami Goldberg and Dan Gruhn have been instrumental in bringing our publications to supporters and benefactors. Their dedication has allowed these ideas to reach far beyond what I could have imagined.

The entire staff of Israel365 contributed in one way or another to this work. I want to thank Shlomo Schreibman, Talia Eisen, Donna Jollay, Zelig Shmuelovitch, Rabbi Mark Fishman, Eliyahu Adam Berkowitz, Sara Lamm, Zahava Schwartz, Mordy Levi, Sharon Michaels, Jeffrey Goldgrab, Inbal Rose, Nissan Lifschitz, Shuey Fogel, Mor Levy, Avraham Perlmutter and Ilan Eshkanazi. Each of you plays a vital role in our mission and it's a pleasure to work with you each day.

After working for so many years primarily with non-Jewish audiences, it was especially gratifying to collaborate closely with passionate Jewish activists who joined Israel365 Action in our World Zionist Congress campaign. Thank you to Shlomo Skaist and Deborah Peretz for reading early drafts and providing thoughtful feedback that improved this work significantly. Thank you to our delegates Tila Levi Falic and Rachael Chevalier, and alternates Irma Fralic and Bruce Jacobson, for your enthusiasm and participation in the first Israel365 Action delegation to the World Zionist Congress. Together, we are working to advance Universal Zionism within the institutional framework that Herzl himself established.

Many ideas in this book were first discussed over delicious Shabbat meals with my lively family. We would start our conversations with the weekly Torah portion, the discussion would inevitably turn to the war these past two years, and then I would always circle back to m favorite topic: Universal Zionism. I am grateful to my children Shaindee, Bella, Dovid, Tzofia, Amitai, Mikey, and Eliyah for your patience in allowing me to test different arguments over and over again and not changing the topic too quickly. The biggest thanks of all goes to my precious wife Abby for giving me time away from family responsibilities just after the birth of our newborn baby to write and most of all, for being a constant source of inspiration and encouragement me.

A final word of appreciation to the God of Israel for the privilege of living today in the Land of Israel and playing a small role in the exciting, unfolding story of the People of Israel. May this book honor the grand vision He has given us and contribute to advancing His glorious plan for Israel and the nations.

BIBLIOGRAPHY

INTRODUCTION

- Kirk, Charlie. *Stop in the Name of God: Why Honoring the Sabbath will Transform Your Life.* Winning Team Publishing. 2025.
- Troy, Gil. *The Zionist Ideas.* The Jewish Publication Society. 2018.
- Mischel, Elie. *The War Against the Bible.* Israel365. 2024.
- Polonsky, Pinchas. *Universal Religious Zionism.*
- Brog, David. *Standing with Israel: Why Christians Support the Jewish State.* Frontline. 2006.

POLITICAL ZIONISM

- Weisz, Georges Yitshak. *Theodor Herzl: A New Reading.* Gefen Publishing House. 2013.
- Hazony, Yoram. *The Jewish State.* Basic Books, 2001.
- Schwartz, Adi and Wilf, Einat. *The War of Return.* All Points Books. 2020.
- Tuchman, Barbara W. *Bible and Sword.* Ballantine Books. 1956.
- Oren, Michael B. *Power, Faith and Fantasy.* Norton & Company, Inc. 2007.

RELIGIOUS ZIONISM

- Druckman, Chaim. *Step by Step: The State of Israel Fulfilling the Vision of our Redemption.* Or Etzion Torah Institute. 2024.
- Naor, Bezalel, translator. *When God Becomes History: Historical Essays of Rabbi Abraham Isaac Hakohen Kook.* Orot, Inc. 2003.
- Saperstein, Marc. *Essential Papers on Messianic Movements and Personalities in Jewish History.* New York University Press. 1992.
- Wolpe, David. *David: The Divided Heart.* Yale University Press. 2014.
- Livni, Abraham. *The Return of Israel and the Hope of the World.* Gefen Books. 2013.

UNIVERSAL ZIONISM

- Israel, Alex. Kings: Torn in Two. Maggid. 2013.

- Pearl, Elisha. *Make Peace: A Strategic Guide for Achieving Lasting Peace In Israel.* Yonah Press. 2024.
- Sacks, Jonathan. *Dignity of Difference.* Continuum. 2002.
- Wald, Shalom Salomon. *Rise and Decline of Civilizations: Lessons for the Jewish People.* The Jewish People Policy Institute. 2014.
- Netanyahu, Benjamin. *A Place Among the Nations: Israel and the World.* Bantam Books. 1993.
- Mischel, Elie. *Shabbat Revolution: A Practical Guide to Weekly Renewal.* Israel365. 2025.

ABOUT THE AUTHOR

Rabbi Tuly Weisz is the founder of Israel365 and the editor of *The Israel Bible*, the first Bible dedicated to highlighting the relationship between the Land and the People of Israel. He also started Israel365 Action, a new party in the advocating for Universal Zionism, Judea and Samaria and stronger relations between Jews and Christians in the World Zionist Congress.

Rabbi Tuly has a regular column, "Unto the Nations" in the *Jerusalem Post* who writes passionately about Israel, the Bible and Jewish-Christian relations. Rabbi Weisz attended Yeshiva University (BA), Rabbi Isaac Elchanan Theological Seminary (Rabbinic Ordination) and the Benjamin Cardozo School of Law (JD) and served as the Rabbi of the Beth Jacob Congregation in Columbus, Ohio before making Aliyah to Israel in 2011. Rabbi Tuly lives with his wife and children in Ramat Beit Shemesh, Israel.

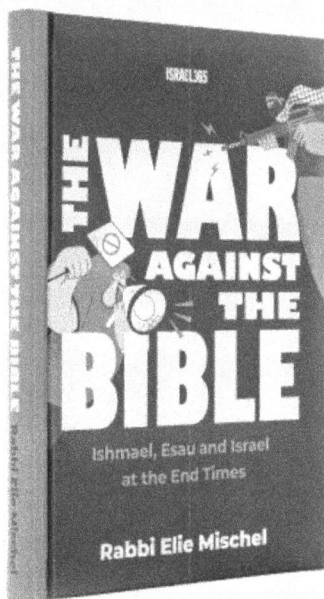

Shut Off the Noise.
Turn On the Divine.

Shabbat Revolution:
A Practical Guide to Weekly Renewal
shows you how to step away from the chaos, unplug with purpose, and create sacred space for God, family, and real peace - **every single week.**

www.ingramcontent.com/pod-product-compliance
Lightning Source LLC
Chambersburg PA
CBHW070103030426
42335CB00016B/1986